SXD488

Published — 2-5-95

CW01395278

1984

COMPULSION

COMPULSION

ROBIN BLAKE & ELEANOR STEPHENS

THAMES

First published in Great Britain in 1987
by Boxtree Limited

Copyright © Thames Television PLC
            Robin Blake and Eleanor Stephens 1987

ISBN 1 85283 208 8

Printed and bound in Great Britain by
Redwood Burn Ltd, Trowbridge, Wiltshire
for Boxtree Limited, 25 Floral Street,
London WC2E 9DS

Song lyrics, composer and author Cole Porter © 1934 Harms Inc.
British publisher Chappel Music Ltd
Used by permission

Contents

For Eliza, Matthew and Nickolas.

Acknowledgments

We are grateful for the work of all the production team on the television series, in particular Mary McAnally, executive producer, researchers, Gill Southcott and Judith Hackett and presenters, Janice Long and Dr Richard Smith; and of course to all the participants who allowed us to share their experiences.

Introduction

People who work in chocolate factories are allowed to eat as much chocolate as they like. That is based on sound psychological principles, because we have in-built mechanisms to make sure that the taste of chocolate quickly cloys and the appetite for it disappears. It is as if there is a control device, something like a thermostat or regulator, with an in-built sense of sufficiency. This switches off our feeling of desire or appetite at the appropriate time, and if this thermostat always worked perfectly, the compulsions we discuss in this book would not exist. But sometimes our sense of what is 'enough' deserts us, and we go on a binge or 'over the top'. Most of us have had experiences like this but for some it becomes a chronic and increasing problem. Understanding such compulsions is the subject of this book.

The compulsions we shall look at are as varied as bingeing on cream cakes, taking tranquillisers or working round the clock. But they all follow similar patterns of a person, usually under pressure or in distress, being compelled by a force they cannot control. The compulsion is strong enough to dominate their life, and it demands to be satisfied even at the expense of the rest of life. So why is it that most people, most of the time, can eat, drink or work to a moderate degree – or a degree which is proportional to the need of the moment – while others feel compelled to go on beyond need and into excess?

Habits, Compulsions, Obsessions

Our motives for doing things are not always conscious, and there are many things we do without really knowing why. Our lives are full of habits which we do not question or attempt to control, simply because our motivation to stop doing them is not strong enough. Nevertheless, whether it is nail-biting, smoking or arguing, we are aware of the habit and feel that, in principle, it is conquerable. We may choose not to control it but, if we had to, we could. It is also noticeable how many habits break themselves naturally when there

1

Compulsion

is a break in our lives – for example, if we go on holiday or change jobs.

At the other end of the spectrum from habits lie obsessions. In the clinical language of psychiatric illness, obsessional neuroses are regarded as symptoms of serious mental disorders, manifesting themselves in obsessional and often ritualised patterns of behaviour and thought. The individual becomes 'stuck' in these repetitions (for example washing their hands endlessly) in such a way as to be entirely divorced from reality. People suffering from these compulsions often have *folie de doute*, where they are beset by fears that their ritual actions have not been carried out satisfactorily, and so must be repeated endlessly. Obsessional neuroses can become so engrossing that they leave little room for normal life, and in this case sufferers need full-time round-the-clock care.

Although they are so different, habits and obsessional neuroses are connected by a common thread – they both consist of repeating actions and thoughts. Our concern, however, is with the area of compulsion, which lies somewhere in between them. Unlike habits, compulsions are not easily broken. Sufferers feel unable to give up the behaviour, however much they would like to. A compulsion is therefore defined, unlike a habit, as a *problem*. It is also, we believe, a sign of more fundamental 'life problems'.

Nevertheless, compulsive drinkers or heroin addicts are not helpless or deluded, as are people caught in the grip of obsessional neurosis. The compulsive lives in the real world, and is able to manipulate it, sometimes with great skill and dedication, in the service of the compulsion. So it is important to remember that compulsive behaviour is in touch with reality, although it is a restricted, narrowly-focused reality.

The compulsion may seem uncontrolled, yet compulsive individuals are not out of control. As we shall see, they are very much *controlled* – under the control of their compulsion. It is as if their normal appetite is overridden whenever they come into contact with the object of the compulsion – a drug, a loved one, a job.

Under such conditions motivation is no longer a matter of judging or choosing between different actions. Everything tends to be evaluated in terms of the compulsion – whether it makes the compulsion easier to follow or otherwise. For this reason it distorts and spoils life because it washes away the rational processes of choice and the repertoire of emotional responses which enrich life.

2

Introduction

Do Compulsions Create Problems or Solve Them?

We have said that compulsive behaviour is by definition a problem. But that is not always the compulsive person's view. It is a matter of common experience that people *take to drink* because of *other* problems in their lives. The drinker in this case uses alcohol as a way of coping with the other problem. The anxious person who is prescribed tranquillisers is in the same position. Both people have, consciously or otherwise, identified difficulties or dilemmas in their lives, and have adopted a form of compulsion as a coping strategy, an attempt, however misguided, to solve their problems. We believe this pattern is common to all forms of compulsive behaviour: beneath the workaholic, anorexic, heroin addict or compulsively jealous marriage partner, there is always a primary problem which underlies the compulsion. This compulsive person *does not see the compulsion as a problem, but as the answer to a problem.*

Yet the compulsion becomes a problem. To see how this happens, compare it with a habit. The habit does not impinge on others, while a compulsion has repercussions throughout our social and emotional lives. It breaks marriages, causes unemployment and destroys friendships. So how can it also be a kind of solution? The creation of problems such as those arising from compulsive behaviour can have several problem-solving aspects. We shall meet two of these, in particular, again and again in the following pages. The first is that a compulsion can conceal the original problem by overlaying it. The compulsion is then a *mask* behind which the person hides his problem from the world and himself. The second sense in which it may be an effective way of coping is as a form of self-punishment, a *lash*. If the sufferer experiences deep-seated feelings of guilt – appropriately or not – then the very serious difficulties which a compulsion brings may be experienced as deserved punishment, an appropriate kind of penance.

There is a common view that becoming compulsive is a sign of weakness, and that people who fall prey to these compulsions lack will-power. The testimonies of the people we have talked to suggest that the opposite is true, that compulsive behaviour often springs from – and often includes – a strong determination to survive under the most difficult circumstances. For example a teenage girl may believe that by controlling her food intake, she can prevent her parents' marriage from disintegrating. Such an action is not a sign of weakness.

Compulsion

Getting Help

In each chapter we shall discuss the variety of help available and the different approaches to treatment and prevention. This variety depends on the variety of theories which are used to account for compulsions. The behaviourist explanation is widely popular, and this means that many types of treatment concentrate on the compulsive behaviour itself, rather than on any underlying problems. It will involve 'rewiring' the 'conditioned responses' which (in the behaviourist's view) alone provide the person's compulsive motivation. One prominent behavioural psychologist Professor H. J. Eysenck, in his book *Fact and Fiction in Psychology*, writes:

> Symptoms are conditioned emotional and motor responses, and ... have no underlying complex infantile origin which gives them their strength. The symptom, as it were, is the illness and the disappearance of the symptom means the disappearance of the illness. Furthermore it is argued that the disappearance of the symptom can be produced by orthodox processes of extinction, very much in the same way as conditioned responses are extinguished every day in the laboratory.

If we substitute 'compulsion' for 'symptom' and 'problem' for 'illness' we have a very fair idea of the behavioural approach to treating compulsive problems such as anorexia and alcohol dependence. As we shall see, it is a process in which the compulsive individual must be cooperative, but is otherwise relatively passive.

Psychotherapy, on the other hand, concentrates on a much more active strategy. It aims at three objectives: to bring out an understanding by the individual of the nature and effect of the compulsion itself; to unearth if possible the underlying meaning of it in his experience; and to find alternative ways to cope. The importance of sufferers' *experiences* (which is not at all the same thing as their *conditioning*) is crucial, and we might illustrate this by reference to the work of Dr R. D. Laing, a psychiatrist who has had a great influence on more humane approaches to mental illness. Emphasising the importance of dealing with a person's experience, Laing wrote: 'If we are stripped of our experience, we are stripped of our deeds; and if our deeds are, so to say, taken out of our hands like toys from the hands of children, we are bereft of our humanity.'

As will be clear, we lean strongly towards the psychotherapeutic appproach, which begins not from an abstract idea of conditioning but from the experience of living. This we believe provides more fruitful and more permanent answers to problems of compulsive behaviour.

At a time when funding for many therapeutic projects is being cut back and resources are scarce it is crucial that sufferers and their families are as well informed as possible about the best kind of help that is available. Often this may be simply a person to talk to, particularly someone who has been through similar experiences. Many self-help groups have been formed with the object of providing this kind of therapy, away from the distant 'objectivity' of many medical people. One woman who was prescribed tranquillisers after a divorce twenty years ago, and has been hooked on them ever since, told us: 'It's taken me twenty years to find someone who would listen to my story. I've thrown away twenty years of my life.' We hope that the information in this book will play a part in making such tragedies less frequent.

The choice of subjects has been limited by time and space, and we regret the omission of several common compulsions such as theft and gambling – though there is some discussion of these and others in the final chapter, where we enlarge on the idea that a full understanding of compulsions depends on an all-round appreciation of the person who suffers from them. It is for this reason that each chapter draws on the first-hand experiences of people who have lived through the different compulsions. We are grateful for their courage in sharing their stories with us, in the belief that it will be of help to others with similar problems.

Chapter 1

Eating

When Jack's a very good boy
He shall have cakes and custard;
But when he does nothing but cry
He shall have nothing but mustard.

Eating is the most basic of human activities and, of course, essential for survival. We are all born with an instinctive compulsion to eat; within moments of birth young mammals start to root for food and the sucking instinct is established very quickly. Through eating, the baby develops an intimacy and closeness with the mother and this bonding lays the foundation for loving relationships in the future.

Yet ironically, for many people, this natural and pleasurable activity becomes a focus of anxieties and conflict, a war zone in which opposing compulsions do battle, sometimes with fatal consequences.

Problems with food are the most common of the compulsions we shall discuss in this book. When we advertised recently for people with different compulsions to contact us, three-quarters of those who replied had problems with eating. Preoccupation with body-weight and body image and an increasing interest in health and nutrition are a feature of modern Western society: as many as 80 per cent of women are either on a diet, have just finished dieting or are about to start a diet. To understand why food should be such a common object of compulsion we need to appreciate the peculiar power which food holds over the social imagination of human beings.

The meaning of food is much wider even than its survival value suggests. Since we are social animals, we feed ourselves through social processes; food ceremonies have acquired deep social and psychological significance, and play a major part in religious ceremonies. Christianity has a symbolic meal, the Mass, as its basic rite, and food-avoidance and fasting are important in the Jewish and Moslem faiths. Meals also play a central role in family life, especially in 'rites of passage' and celebrations: the christening cake, the wedding breakfast, the funeral wake, Easter eggs, the Thanksgiving turkey and the Christmas dinner.

Food can also carry very personal messages. The candlelit dinner may be an expression of romantic love; and the offering of a box of chocolates is thought – by advertisers at least – to be a seduction technique. Eating together is also central to important political and business deals. In Turkey they still kill and cook a sheep over the foundations of every new building.

The social meaning of food is so important to us that making sure our children have good table manners and can eat appropriately is one of the great aims of pre-school training, and the table is one of the earliest arenas of conflict between parent and child. It is therefore not surprising that when conflicts arise in later life, our eating pattern – our *relationship* with food – often reflects our problematic emotions and relations with other people.

For many sufferers from compulsive eating problems, food becomes a vehicle for an unconscious signalling of important messages. In the stories that follow, all told to us by real people (some of whose names we have changed), we will try to unravel some of those messages.

Gill's Story

Gill Cox is agony aunt to readers of a well-known women's magazine and receives letters from thousands of women who pour out their desire to control their weight or break repetitive cycles of compulsive bingeing and stringent dieting. Her sympathetic responses are particularly poignant in that she herself has experienced ten years of eating problems.

For many people the late teens and early twenties are a time of exhilaration, creativity and discovery. For Gill, many of these discoveries were painful ones. She would not have known or accepted at first the label of 'compulsive eater': she was just the child whom they nicknamed 'Michelin'.

For Gill, now an attractive 35-year-old of average build, used to be fat. Her mother, she told us, had always had a weight problem of her own, and Gill wonders if she has inherited it – or at least (as she put it) 'the psychology to get a weight problem'. When she was about thirteen she started to be self-conscious about being fat, and so began the long cycle of bingeing and dieting which dominated her eating over the next decade. She must have tried every regime in every book, she thinks: from total fasting to the grapefruit diet, the egg diet, the Cambridge Diet and cottage cheese 'till it came out of my ears'. Some of these were even quite successful. At sixteen, for instance, she was able to get down to her target ideal weight.

But it never lasted. Gill would stick to that target weight for a few weeks, and then find herself raiding the biscuit tin or stuffing with chocolates. She would start a diet on a Monday having, on the preceding Sunday, deliberately gorged on all the foods she intended to deny herself. This was all very secretive. She lied to her friends, inventing a metabolic problem to account for the relapses after every diet. 'I told them I only had to look at a cake to put on pounds. But in reality I was eating double portions in the canteen and chocolates between meals.'

Curiously, her mother was a secret accomplice. 'I now know that my mother knew I was raiding the biscuit tin (she was the one who filled it!) and that she found all my sweet-papers – but she still patiently fed me my weight-watcher's jelly!'

Gill believes that her lack of confidence about being with other people, especially boyfriends, was at the root of her problem. Fatness became her alibi 'so that I didn't have to say no, I didn't have to make decisions – they were made for me.'

At nineteen Gill left home and set herself up in her own flat. Quite quickly her weight problem got out of control, for now she could indulge herself much more freely. She reached fifteen stone and began to have bouts of severe depression. Then, suddenly, she saw herself as if from the outside, as others must see her. This was after the arrival of young woman at her place of work who, Gill thought, must have been anorexic. 'She had a cottage cheese and brown crispbread obsession, that was all she ate and that was all she talked about. I suddenly realised how boring I must have seemed to all my friends ... And I remember walking up the stairs in a flat I was in, having got another bowl of porridge and another handful of digestive biscuits thinking "why am I doing this to myself?" And realising that you're doing it to yourself, and that's it's not a lack of will-power – the will is to eat!'

Gradually the compulsive circle of bingeing and dieting began to grow weaker. At the same time Gill's social life was improving, her horizons widening. She felt more confident, better able to deal with men friends. Today, in her mid thirties, she has completely given up dieting and has remained the same weight since the age of twenty-five.

Gill found that dieting led to an obsession with the foods she tried to give up. She believes compulsive eaters use weight as a barrier and as a statement. 'Being fat is somehow linked to being naughty – I wasn't consciously rebelling against society, but I was determined not to get into the "nice girl" pattern which was adhered to by my mother: nice girls settle down and get married at twenty: I didn't want to do that, so I got fat.'

Gill's compulsive eating resolved itself once she gained some insight into why she was doing it – an essential element in any effort to break out from a circle of compulsive behaviour. For those who cannot break out, the pattern of bingeing and self-starvation becomes so extreme that it seriously threatens their health and happiness.

Anorexia and Bulimia

Anorexia and bulimia are two sides of the same coin. The full medical name *anorexia nervosa* means, literally, a nervous loss of appetite. *Bulimia nervosa* is the opposite, an insatiable appetite. It is easy to see therefore that bulimia is compulsive in a straightforward sense, since sufferers are possessed by an inner drive to eat more than is good for them. But how is *anorexia nervosa* a compulsion, since having no appetite seems rather a negative state – the lack, in fact, of what is (under proper control) a perfectly normal compulsion?

In fact, anorexia is very much more than a lack of desire for food, and it is misleading to think of anorexia and bulimia simply as opposites. In people suffering from psychological eating disorders the coin's two sides – a desire to overeat and to resist eating – often fall uppermost together, creating a psychological paradox, and an agonising conflict for the sufferer.

A variety of instinctive myths and beliefs have grown up around these eating disorders and food compulsions. Some regard bulimia as mere greed and lack of self-control. From a similar moralistic point of view, compulsive dieting may seem no more than vanity – slimming that has gone 'a bit too far'. Many people believe that anorexia is actually caused by particular techniques of slimming or by the slimming process itself. It is also widely considered to be a problem that only young women have. We shall hope to find all these myths demolished by the end of the chapter. But first, how widespread is the problem?

Compulsion

An Epidemic?

There is no question that the subject of psychological eating disorders takes up much more medical time and thought now than it did before the Second World War. Research among schoolchildren has shown that, in private girls' schools, one in 100 of the pupils over sixteen had anorexia. In the young female population as a whole the anorexia rate is lower, but at about one in 200 it is still extremely worrying, especially since a small number of anorexics die from self-starvation.

These are, of course, cases notified to doctors and are therefore the most serious. Other research shows the enormous amount of weight-watching in our population, much of it at a near-anorexic level. Susie Orbach, author of *Fat Is A Feminist Issue*, told us that a third of women in their late teens and early twenties control their weight through vomiting, fluid-reducing drugs, laxatives or periodic fasting. Each of these is an extreme and unnatural method of slimming, and their use suggests that extreme and unnatural anxiety about weight is very much more widespread than we might imagine from the medical statistics. Nor are all sufferers young women: Susie Orbach has treated grandmothers in their sixties, and male anorexics.

Statistics, in any case, can tell us little about how it feels to have these compulsions. There is no 'typical' case: all cases are different. But a good deal can be discovered about these complex problems from people's own life-stories.

Elaine's Story

Elaine is four foot ten and twenty-eight years old. But she looks and dresses much younger. It was at twenty, whilst working as a medical receptionist, that she discovered how dieting made her feel happy and more glamorous. As she became thinner she felt more confident, more relaxed and in the first year she was delighted to have got her weight down to four and a half stone.

Elaine's only food by this time was a single tin of rice pudding per day, which she would put aside and eat just before bedtime. She found this food easiest to swallow. But like many anorexics, Elaine was not initially debilitated by her drastic weight loss. If anything, she was invigorated. She walked everywhere and swam in her local pool each morning at seven. For the first time she felt powerful and in control of her life.

10

However she was becoming increasingly isolated. She gave up her job and spent more and more time alone. Then she began losing some of her iron control. She would eat whole bags of sweets and chocolates, before reasserting her will by making herself vomit. It was not until she had heart palpitations in the middle of the night that she suddenly became frightened. She went to her doctor and so began the years of lonely and painful treatment. Now she is better, and hopes to train as a therapist specialising in anorexia and bulimia.

Michelle's Story

Michelle is twenty-eight, like Elaine, and the mother of a baby son. She lives with her baby's father in a Victorian house in the north of England, is self-employed, and enjoys her work as a psychotherapist. A settled existence.

Yet it was only two years ago that Michelle gave up the habit of making herself vomit every time she ate. For nine years prior to that her life had been dominated by a compulsion to binge on food, to eat voraciously – especially sweet things, fats and carbohydrates. Like many bulimics, she found the normal orderly pattern of three meals a day was destroyed, and she found herself at the mercy of chaotic and unpredictable urges. The only way she felt able to control her weight was to vomit the food up immediately: at the height of her compulsion, Michelle was spending hundreds of pounds on food every month, and making herself sick eight or nine times a day. Then, after almost a decade of this behaviour, which she had struggled bravely to combat through counselling, psychiatric treatment and spells in hospital, the compulsion faded. Now, at last, Michelle feels she is well on the way to recovery.

The physical effects for Elaine and Michelle were serious. Michelle's weight fluctuated wildly. She suffered bouts of severe depression, and needed tranquillisers. She made two suicide attempts. She developed a condition called tetany – continual muscle spasms and cramps caused by calcium deficiency. Elaine, too, suffered uncomfortable physical side effects. She had palpitations and sweats. She often felt cold, especially in the hands and feet. Her periods stopped entirely when her weight fell below five stone. But worst of all were the depressions which hit Elaine terribly under the pressure of treatment, and the stress she felt as her weight gradually increased.

Compulsion

One way to think of cases like these might be as *appetitive disorders*, diseases of the appetite *mechanism*. In order to understand whether this is appropriate we need to look at what 'normal' appetite is and how it is acquired.

Hunger and Appetite

Although in everyday language to be hungry and have an appetite mean much the same thing, the two are not the same. Appetite is the motive force that makes us eat, while hunger is the physical effect of *not* eating. Of course, real hunger can also prompt us to take food, but by then we are already suffering from the effect of not having eaten. The sugar balance in the bloodstream is disturbed and there are stomach contractions. This is the meaning of the 'gnawing' of hunger.

Appetite, of course, turns us all into compulsives, since it is designed to preempt hunger pangs by creating, at appropriate moments, a powerful urge to eat. This usually happens well before the unpleasant effects of undernourishment begin, and, unlike hunger, it is not on the whole an unpleasant sensation. Appetite is controlled not in the stomach itself, but from a location in the brain called the hypothalamus, which acts as a sort of command post for many of the body's automatic processes.

Everyone knows that illness interferes with appetite: in a fever, for instance, we don't feel much like eating. The secretion of gastric juices is greatly cut down at an early stage of illness, when all the body's resources are concentrated on combatting the infection. So, in recognition of the priorities of the situation, appetite is shut down. Stress and distress, or, as we shall see in a later chapter, heightened emotional states like falling in love, may also cause a loss of appetite; the hypothalamus is part of the brain's emotional centre, and therefore emotional disturbances may, as a side-effect, switch off the appetite.

There is another crucial defining characteristic of appetite which distinguishes it from hunger: it is not an inborn response. Hunger happens automatically when a critical threshold of undernourishment is crossed, signalled by chemical changes in the bloodstream. So it is caused by the body's actual and immediate need for food. Appetite is not triggered by any absolute need: it must anticipate need, and therefore it has to be *learned*.

Eating

Learning and Food

Learning explains how unconnected sights, sounds, tastes and smells stimulate appetite, even though they have no necessary connection with nutritious eating. Obviously the most powerful and universal signals *are* to do with food preparation: the smell of fresh bread, the sound of bacon sizzling under the grill, a chef glimpsed carving a juicy roast. But, as even these examples show, it is not merely the food itself which causes us to want to eat, but all the incidental things surrounding food and eating.

Almost anything, if we learn to connect it with food, is capable of making us feel hungry. The pioneer Russian psychologist Ivan Pavlov proved this almost 100 years ago when he showed that, by presenting a hungry dog with food and, simultaneously, with the sound of a bell, you could condition the dog to salivate just by ringing the bell. Salivation is one of those automatic responses which, like appetite, is controlled in the brain, and although Pavlov had no way of asking his dogs if, as well as salivating, they also felt hungry whenever the bell rang, it is virtually certain that they did. Almost any stimulus may become powerfully associated with eating or hunger (especially if the association is established at an early age) and can set in motion powerful compulsive feelings to eat.

Pavlov called this process conditioning. Today psychologists are more likely to talk about a *learned* rather than a *conditioned* response, but the principle is essentially the same, and it is by this principle that we learn appetite. We learn in particular when to eat, the pattern of meals and the kinds of meals to expect at breakfast, lunch and tea. The appetite we feel at around midday has little to do with hunger: it is our conditioning telling us to expect a meal. From the point of view of evolution, such learning is clearly useful, since we need appetite to ensure a healthy and regular food intake.

We also learn aversion and even disgust at unfamiliar foods, and this too is necessary to avoid what may be harmful. This is why we may feel physical disgust at the thought of many dishes which – in other cultures – are extraordinary delicacies. In Britain or America few will share the bedouin tribesman's savour for the sheep's eye and the ram's testicle. Virtually all our ideas about what makes food especially delicious and desirable develop according to the region and the kind of society in which we live. This is where we learn about eating, and we eat according to how we have learned.

13

Compulsion

What Causes Eating Disorder?

Our conditioning, as we have already seen, is overridden in some ordinary illnesses, so that when, for instance, we go down with flu, the appetite for food temporarily deserts us. Certain diseases, like cancer, can lead to chronic loss of appetite; others, like diabetes, may make us want to eat to excess.

Once organic disease is ruled out, we are left only with psychological explanations. As we have seen in the Introduction, behavioural psychologists like H. J. Eysenck tend to regard addictions as diseases of the mind, where psychological mechanisms such as association and conditioning have broken down or become disordered. A behaviourist begins with the facts as we have already established them: appetite is a learned (or, in their terms, a *conditioned*) reflex. If it is not working properly this must be because the conditioning process has gone wrong and the wires have become crossed. So, according to this view, there is no need to enquire into the childhood and emotional background of the patient, as is clear from the words quoted from Eysenck in the Introduction. Mental disorders are more like arbitrary, even accidental events, little to do with the patient's detailed life history. They can best be disentangled by psychological readjustment – or, if we use computer terms, reprogramming. We shall learn a little about what this means for treatment later on.

Taking an almost diametrically opposite view are therapists such as Susie Orbach, who see eating or dieting compulsions not as negative and involuntary states, but as positive and voluntary ones. Susie Orbach told us that 'the young anorexic woman, who doesn't feel good inside of herself, who's not proud of who she is, creates somebody out of herself, somebody she can admire, somebody who doesn't have needs.' Eating problems are seen as a response to underlying dilemmas, an attempt, however misguided, to cope with primary life problems, as we have called them. Michelle's bulimia has been described above largely in terms of what happened to her, the objective facts. But for therapists like Orbach, it is essential also to understand the emotional background. Only when sufferers develop some insight into their own emotional geography can they start to navigate the long road to recovery.

Michelle Again

This emotional landscape is almost invariably one of deprivation. Michelle's experiences and feelings, for example, will strike a chord with many other sufferers from food compulsions. Her parents split up when she was ten and along with four younger brothers and sisters she was put into a children's home. When her father re-married, she went to live with him, but she realised that her stepmother hated her while her father played the tyrant. By fifteen, Michelle started shop-lifting, and eventually spent two more years in a children's home, terrified that she would one day have to return to her father. Her father told social workers that she was promiscuous and she had even been put on the Pill whilst at the home.

Michelle's dominant emotions were loneliness and a feeling that she was worthless. Her emotional insecurity continued into adult life, in spite of her achieving considerable academic success, and a place at university. Boyfriends were a problem because she could never accept that she was loved or desired for herself. Hence her depression and suicide attempts. Seen against this background, her adoption of binge eating and vomiting fits our view of this kind of compulsion – that far from being an irrational weakness, it is an understandable course of conduct, chosen under great pressure and requiring a special kind of lonely and heroic dedication.

Elaine's hermit-like existence and her self-discipline over food showed the same qualities. Her *happiness* in the first stages of self-starvation is a paradox, but it came in part from the fact that through dieting she found for the first time a sense of control over her own life. This element of *control* is central to eating and dieting compulsions, and we shall return to it. For the moment we would simply point out how seriously it undermines strictly behaviourist 'crossed-wire' theories about food compulsions.

Anorexia and Men

Anorexia is commonly regarded as a woman's problem or, to borrow the title of Orbach's book, an exclusively *feminist issue*. This is a misconception. While it is true that most anorexics and bulimics are female, about 10 per cent are male and have similar stories to tell. Dave is one.

Dave's Story

Dave thinks his anorexia stems back to a time eight years before it appeared. His parents were divorced when he was eight, after his father had left and begun to live with another woman. 'He visited us, my younger brother and I, once a fortnight, and I found this very threatening and unsettling.' Dave was a school sports star, but 'I remember sports day as being very traumatic because Mum and Dad would be at opposite ends of the track and I would feel I'd have to share my happiness half with my Mum and half with Dad.'

In spite of his sporting prowess, Dave felt he was bullied at school. By the time he was thirteen financial difficulties had forced him and his brother to leave their private school and be sent to different state schools. Now Dave began to withdraw into himself. He used his favourite sports events, running and swimming, as alibis because they 'meant I didn't have to come into contact with too many people'. At the age of sixteen Dave was over six foot, but weighed only five and a half stone. A family friend suggested he might be anorexic. Under treatment, he was told he must eat more and cut down on his stringent exercise programme. But, he says, 'I was very reluctant to eat more and eat the right things; food was the one thing I had previously had control of in my life.'

Numbers of intertwined strands of guilt, fear, disgust and self-accusation lurk in the background of many stories like Dave's. Disrupted family life seems to be particularly common among anorexics – it is a feature, for instance, of all the cases discussed in this chapter. A sense of personal *responsibility* for what happens and of the need to maintain control are particularly prominent. Sometimes the compulsion (whether anorexia or bulimia) appears as a form of self-punishment, with the sufferers blaming themselves for things that have happened – either for causing or for failing to prevent them. And Dave, echoing Elaine, said that 'food was the one thing I had previously had control of in my life'. It looks as if Dave started his food compulsion in order to give himself the certainty of control, in a world where he had previously felt conspicuously unable to manage events in his family. This supports the explanation put forward in the Introduction that compulsion develops as a coping strategy to deal with underlying, primary problems.

Another interesting aspect of Dave's story is his exercise obsession. The compulsion to exercise is particularly common among male anorexics, though it exists in some females too. It involves pushing yourself to the very limits with punishing fitness regimes. The stereotype of the superfit sportsman can easily become a male equivalent of the rake-thin fashion model, each a supposedly desirable model for young people in this society. Doctors are now seeing compulsive exercisers of both sexes more frequently than in the past, and find that the problem is very similar to eating disorders, as it too is concerned with body-weight and body image. The compulsive exerciser can never accept that he is fit enough; anorexics often have a distorted body image, making them think they are much fatter than they really are.

But it is the extreme and dedicated self-destructiveness of anorexia which seems particularly baffling. Anorexia is a hard and inflexible taskmaster, and every anorexic's story is one of intense moral pain. But few play more tragic and painful variations on the theme than Catherine Dunbar.

Catherine's Story

Catherine's life can be read in her mother Maureen's moving book *Catherine*, which was published in 1986. It is a harrowing tale of self-destruction under iron control. She was the third child of the marriage. Her father John, a self-made investment analyst, had come from a Merseyside council house to the home counties and acquired a life-style to match. The children had private schooling and a private swimming-pool, and were happy and united. Then it began to go wrong. In Catherine's early teens, John Dunbar's business life started to come apart. He was moody and intro-spective, stayed in bed for whole weekends, and drank heavily.

Catherine had been sent to boarding school. She had wanted to go, but a part of her protested against it. Once established there, her protest took the sinister form of a hunger strike. Eventually she became so thin that she needed to be admitted to hospital, where under a behaviourist regime of 'rewards and punishments' (which we shall look at later) her weight went back to the target of eight stone. Her mental state was lonely and disturbed, but she began to do well academically, passing four 'O' Levels. Yet by now the refusal of food had for her become a way of life, and for the next five years she was in and out of hospital – having her weight built up, only to leave and let it drop once more. Apart from chronic fasting, Catherine also suffered from intense periodic bingeing followed by laxatives. These she took with the dedication of an addict, so that by the age of twenty she was swallowing 100 tablets a day. She began to talk of no longer wanting to live. Catherine's mother (who in the meantime had left John Dunbar and, after three

17

months, returned) fed her baby food and for a while they achieved a body-weight of five stone.

Catherine made attempts to live a normal life. She found a job as a nanny, but then suddenly took an overdose. After a second suicide bid and a further spell in hospital, Catherine let her weight get down to a level so low that she was clearly dying of starvation. She died when she was twenty-two.

Maureen Dunbar thinks her daughter unconsciously chose anorexia as a way of life, so that soon she could no longer imagine life without it, although at another level she hated it and struggled to be free of it. In the end, the only way she *could* be free was in death.

Compulsion and Will

One of the common characteristics of compulsive people is the unconscious desire to punish themselves for their inability to control or affect bad situations in the family. This seemed to be a part of Catherine's problem – did she feel guilty at her 'desertion' in going away to school? But all compulsive behaviours show many facets, many hidden motives. They are like diabolic recipes with many ingredients – elements in the upbringing, family circumstances, the age of the person, emotional insecurity, availability of outside friendship, the need for love.

In another of their aspects, compulsions turn, not inwards against the sufferer, but outwards towards other people. Anorexic or bulimic young people want to *say* something about themselves. Their actions often translate into a kind of manifesto written in body language, a desperate attempt to change their tangled social and emotional situations. The adoption of damaging compulsive behaviour shows how hard they are prepared to work in pursuit of the objective. They go to the limits of endurance, put themselves at extreme risk and even, as in Catherine's case, sometimes choose to die for it.

Peter Pan's Dilemma

Food can become a vehicle for unconsciously signalling various kinds of message, and one of the most common is that of Peter Pan:

> PETER (*passionately*) I don't want to go to school and learn solemn things. No one is going to catch me, lady, and make me a man. I want always to be a little boy and to have fun.

J. M. Barrie knew that he was tapping a universal theme when he wrote this; he knew, too, that it was an unconscious double-cross, for when he published the play, he placed the following stage direction under it: '(So perhaps he thinks, but it is only his greatest pretend.)' The internal conflicts which arise from attempts to deny the undeniable – the onset of sexual maturity and adulthood – are among the most common causes of food compulsions, and certainly help to explain why they start when they do, during or just after the teenage years.

As in the nursery jingle at the head of this chapter, food is often used to communicate moral judgements and emotions to children and, in response to this, toddlers themselves often make a big issue of food. In the families of anorexics and bulimics food may well have been treated as an especially emotive early symbol. It was like that for Catherine: her mother was liberal, feeling there was no sense in forcing her daughter (always a very choosy eater) to finish her meals; her father, on the other hand, was authoritarian, often attempting to *make* his daughter eat up. When, ten years later, the emotional climate of the family deteriorated into open conflict between Catherine's parents, this memory of old battles reasserted itself. Instead of some more conventional adolescent type of rebellion, Catherine chose to adopt a toddler's mode of defiance.

Where there is this unconscious resistance to the idea of growing up, the physical effects of anorexia in particular will strongly reinforce it. It is not merely that starvation makes the person weaker and more dependent, though this is also true. Below five stone, menstruation stops, secondary sexual characteristics like breasts and pubic hair start to disappear, and the skin even begins to regrow the very fine body hair (known medically as *lanugo*) which covers the human foetus and can still be seen on small children. Thus a twenty-year-old woman can return to the physical state, and weight, of a five-year-old child.

At the same time, the little food that the anorexic *can* eat falls in line with childhood eating. We remember Elaine with her tinned rice pudding, and Catherine, whose mother fed her purees and baby food.

The pathos of all this is increased in the light of the emotional history of many of these sufferers. Elaine, whose father died when she was fourteen, was, as far as she can remember, shown no parental love as a child. Her compulsion seems in essence to have been an attempt to *get back* to childhood, as if to have a second chance. Dave – bullied and lonely – took twenty years to recover from his parents' divorce when he was eight. Michelle, the bulimic, could not accept the love of other people: but at the back of *her* emotional disturbance lurked something much more sinister than the teenage blues. It was not until her mid-twenties, in the throes of psychotherapy, that she dredged up her long-suppressed memories of her father's violence and sexual abuse.

Dreams and Delusions

Anorexics and bulimics are high achievers. All those discussed in this chapter were successful pupils with good academic records. Emotionally they set themselves high standards, impossibly high. The dream of perfection, that state of childlike appearance, of immaculate thinness, possesses them. The primitive or animal urge to gorge uncontrollably on food is an ever-present horror with them.

Another dream is of a perfect dominance over the enemy – food. This can take the form of an obsessive interest in cookery, even in nutrition. Anorexics are sometimes tireless in trying to get other people to eat. Hours may be spent in preparation of meals for the family – never for themselves. Anorexics and bulimics loathe eating in public. If forced into it they become as skilled as magicians in *seeming* to eat, whilst all the time slipping food into a napkin on their lap, or hiding it under a piece of lettuce or cutlery on the plate. All these aspects of the compulsion are part of the need to exercise control. Perfection *is* perfect control.

The delusions are even more bewildering. Anorexics have little appreciation of their real physical state. While others see them as walking skeletons, they look in the mirror and see a gross and bloated person. The delusions always make sure that the dream is pushed firmly out of reach.

Getting Well

Finding help is not a delusion, although, as Catherine's story shows, anorexia can be an extremely dangerous state. In the spectrum of treatment which exists for these compulsions there are two contrasting approaches – behavioural treatment and psychotherapy.

Although we have made it clear that we do not think the behaviourist explanation for eating and dieting compulsions really fits the experience of these disorders, there are still hospitals which offer the kind of 'reprogramming' treatment which assumes that they derive from inappropriate conditioning. In these cases, the aim of reprogramming is to bury the inappropriate learned responses under new, more appropriate ones. These treatments are often known as behaviour modification.

Punishments and Rewards

An extreme form of behavioural therapy for anorexia will typically try to remove the inappropriate response – the food phobia – as if by coercion. This is done in just the way a dog is trained, by a system of rewards for good responses (appropriate eating habits) and punishments for bad ones. Crude punitive treatment was common in the psychiatry of two centuries ago, when the mentally ill were often beaten, straitjacketed and locked in solitary confinement for 'bad' behaviour. Such harsh treatment was never conspicuously successful, and today's punishments take the relatively milder form of a withdrawal of privileges – the right to wear clothes, to watch television, even to go to the lavatory. Formally, of course, the patient's agreement to the reward/ punishment scheme is asked for. But how sincere and informed this consent is at the start of treatment must always be open to question.

Dr Chris Evans of St George's Hospital in London told us how he uses modified behavioural therapy as part of his treatment of people with bulimic eating problems. His first objective is to help them to recognise what their behaviour is. As we have already noted, this is not as difficult as with anorexia. Patients are asked to monitor and record their eating, bingeing and vomiting habits and to record, too, any thoughts, feelings and actions which they think may be associated with the compulsion. An initial ten weeks of intense therapy is followed up by a second stage in which patients attend the hospital every three months.

Usually, Dr Evans believes, bulimia sufferers can be effectively treated as out-patients, but they are sometimes admitted to hospital, as Michelle was. Occasionally these admissions might be made compulsorily under Section 2 of the Mental Health Act (the process which patients know as being 'sectioned'). This is much more likely to happen to anorexics. Elaine was threatened with sectioning, and it was this, she believes, that frightened her into making herself better.

Whether through sectioning or not, severe anorexia almost inevitably involves a stay in a hospital bed. At St George's a form of reprogramming is, again, the essential objective. First a diet is prescribed, with an essential carbohydrate component – Dr Evans believes this is necessary because anorexics particularly avoid carbohydrates. Next, targets of bodily weight and meal timings are identified, so that a weight-increase curve is worked out which will eventually achieve an ideal weight based on the sufferer's weight before the problem began. Almost the whole spectrum of psychological therapies may then be used to establish and reinforce new learned responses – psychodrama, group therapy, art therapy and so on. The patient is treated rather like someone with a phobia – gradually introduced to things such as eating in company, and talking about food in a non-obsessional way.

Psychotherapy

Psychotherapist Susie Orbach's approach starts at the other end of the problem. She is adamant that the compulsion itself is not the problem; rather it is a kind of solution to all the other problems in the person's life: the problems of need and control, of the desire for love and affection and self-worth. For these food is merely the most powerful metaphor to hand, and so becomes an instrument of self-expression or even self-destruction.

She believes that to focus from the start on the need to gain weight is to miss the point. A battle of wills over eating is, for the therapist, a losing battle. It is one which the anorexic relishes far more than he or she can relish the prescribed hospital food.

So Susie Orbach's therapy concentrates on listening and understanding: understanding the individual's own story and especially those childhood years to which so many problem eaters seem bent on returning; understanding, too, of the wider society, in which food and body-shape are such major issues, in which the idea of fatness has become dangerous for women and the tyranny of fashion has made outsiders of so many.

This understanding is the key to grasping the force of other compulsions discussed in this book. Food compulsions, like drugs or work, are both a mask and a lash. When young persons feel unsure of who they are or how they will turn out, they may grasp at food as an idea and a symbol of what they might become and as a means of attaining it. By denying your need for food you symbolically deny all your other needs. By controlling your food intake you can have the feeling of controlling your life. In this mask you are strong and resolute, alone and powerful against the world.

You may also use food as a lash to punish yourself for imaginary crimes and failings, or for the problems of those you love, thereby fulfilling that sense of unworthiness which you have always experienced from childhood.

Self-Help

The insight which constitutes the first step towards recovery is often best gained by actively sharing experiences with other sufferers, and this is the basis of the self-help approach to treatment. Self-help groups also encourage their members to come to terms with the primary problems which have led them to adopt the compulsion as well as the difficulties caused by the compulsion itself. People who are wrestling with compulsions often have tremendous feelings of failure and isolation: 'I never believed there was anyone else with my problem' is a common refrain. So meeting other sufferers and sharing support can be immensely therapeutic and inspiring. There are about fifty self-help groups for people with eating problems all over Britain, and there are some contact addresses at the end of this book.

Anorexic Aid

Anorexic Aid functions as a network of voluntary self-help groups and is run by people who have suffered with anorexia and bulimia. It was started in 1974 after an article in a Sunday newspaper prompted more than 500 letters from people desperately needing help. Renee Botham, a former anorexic and vice-chairman of Anorexic Aid, told us how sufferers often need to reach 'rock bottom' before turning for help. This is similar to one of the concepts used by Alcoholics Anonymous to describe the state of a compulsive drinker who comes to them in need of help.

The group process encourages people to come to terms with the hopeless state they have reached and then, with support and understanding, to start rebuilding their lives. This can take months or years, but for many people it is still more effective than individual medical treatment. Others find that self-help is an invaluable way of following up their conventional treatment and prevents them from falling back into compulsive eating patterns.

Anorexic Family Aid

The food compulsion, like all the others we are discussing, is a problem not just for sufferers, but also for their family and friends.

Yet as Maureen, Catherine's mother, told us, the family often do not spot the warning signs or, if they do, they are quite unable to deal with these complex, destructive problems. They also suffer enormous guilt, which only makes matter worse.

Anorexic Family Aid exists to provide information about eating problems and where to go for help. It runs a telephone hotline service, listed at the end of the book.

Chapter 2

Drinking

Thirst not after that frothy liquor ale; for who knows when he openeth the stopple what may be in the bottle? *Ben Jonson*

Drinking alcohol is something that 96 per cent of the adult population does, whether it is the occasional glass of sherry or several pints of beer in a day. You only have to watch almost any television drama or soap opera to see what a central part drinking alcohol plays in our society – where would *Coronation Street* be without the Rover's Return? Around the world, alcohol is produced and consumed in greater quantities each year, and is generally thought to be a pleasurable and desirable indulgence. Yet this reputation is something of a mystery, since alcohol is physically a very dangerous substance, with many far from pleasant side effects.

The stomach and the liver are worst affected by long-term heavy drinking. The tissue is permanently inflamed, which leads to scarring, chronic gastritis and cirrhosis. In full-blown cirrhosis the liver has gradually been converted almost entirely to fibrous scar tissue. Eventually the kidneys are damaged, and the heart also, for there is a slow replacement of heart muscle by fatty tissue. This is why heavy drinkers often die prematurely of heart failure. These physical effects are fairly well known. Others are less so. A recent report by the Royal College of Physicians stated that alcohol causes infertility in the male. At one clinic, out of sixty-seven patients examined, forty were infertile as a result of alcohol consumption. Nor would they be regarded as heavy drinkers – the majority drank only two or three pints of beer a day.

The effects of alcohol consumption on society generally are also extremely sobering. Statistics about crime, accidents and money spent on alcohol-related problems (£2 billion in the UK in 1985) make one realise that the scope of the harm caused by this powerful drug is very wide indeed. So what is it, and how does it affect us?

Compulsion

What is Alcohol?

Ethyl alcohol – the active ingredient of alcoholic drinks – is a chemical with the formula C^2H^5OH. It is the product of the process of fermentation, which simply means the action of yeast converting sugar into alcohol. Even a tiny dose of this chemical has some effect. As it passes into the bloodstream directly through the stomach walls it causes irritation and swelling in the mucus membranes of the stomach lining. It quickly disseminates itself evenly throughout the body fluids (which make 70 per cent of our weight) and immediately begins its most blatant function: that of *depressing the action of cells*. Its ability to do this explains why, in sufficient quantities, alcohol is a poison. It can effectively anaesthetise you to death by shutting down all vital activity.

Of course taking alcohol in such large doses has little to offer the majority of us, unless we are feeling seriously suicidal. What we look for in a drink is a *smaller* dose of the drug, to bring about a *little* depression of the body's cells and a pleasureable mood change.

In these lesser doses alcohol has more significant effects on humans than on other species. This is because the cells most sensitive to its depressive activity are the brain cells, of which (relative to our body weight) we have more than other animals. And the most subtle of the brain cells are the first to be affected: those which handle self-criticism, worry, judgement, concentration, self-control. Your performance of a task is *never* improved by a drink, except in the sense that it depresses parts of the brain that inhibit you, that cause you, for example, to *think* before you act. This can in some circumstances be a small advantage – socially at least, since you appear more spontaneous and less hesitant than you otherwise might. However any activity that requires precision – driving springs to mind – is adversely affected from the very first sip of alcohol.

So why *is* this pleasant? It can only be because if you remove inhibition, self-criticism and self-doubt you have instant liquid liberation, a holiday from the restrictive side of your own personality. Now you can do things you could not do before, go places that you had never dared enter, become close to people who would once have seemed like strangers; adopt the roles so widely exploited by alcohol advertising.

This is why alcohol is the classic recreational drug, and for most people most of the time it is harmless, even life-enhancing. But alcohol is a drug, and the more you use it the more you depend on it. For certain people, the 'holiday' becomes a compulsory journey into exile, degradation and even early death.

Insults to the Brain

One night in 1953 in New York, the poet Dylan Thomas came back to the apartment where he was staying and told his hosts he had downed eighteen straight whiskies in a single session and boasted 'I think that's the record.' Shortly afterwards he lapsed into a coma from which he never recovered. The coroner's report stated simply that he had died of an 'insult to the brain'. Some drinkers use alcohol as a weapon of violence against themselves. Their drinking is in bouts, great quantities consumed in single sessions or sprees perhaps lasting days. This pattern of drinking is the technical meaning of 'dipsomania'. It is often accompanied by angry speech and violent behaviour and can be so frightening to witness that it seems likely to stem from deliberate and extreme self-hatred. There are often quite long sober periods between such episodes, until a sufferer 'falls off the wagon' and disappears once more into his or her chosen hell.

This kind of drinking compulsion is very sharply defined. It is like bulimia in its suddenness and in its voraciousness, in the way the drinker dreads its reappearance between bouts, and most of all perhaps the self-loathing and remorse afterwards.

Such alcoholics are the battered aristocrats of the world of compulsive drinking. A certain amount of (undeserved) glamour attaches to them, while at the same time they are the most unmistakeable 'criers out for help', the starkest stereotypes of alcoholism. But in spite of the medical dangers of their sudden bouts, they are not necessarily as seriously at risk as certain other problem drinkers. Just as deep-seated – and much more insidious – is the drinking compulsion of those for whom all day every day a steady drip of alcohol flows through the bloodstream.

For such people alcohol is a structural component of their life blood. While the bout drinker may go without a drink for weeks or months on end, the chronic drinker cannot exist from hour to hour without a measure of alcohol in the body. The bout drinker can mark the sharp difference between two types of behaviour – drunk and sober. The chronic drinker has forgotten the difference, like Spencer Tracy, who claimed to have been drunk for twenty-five years. Indeed, in the life histories of people who have developed chronic alcohol dependence, the transition from one state to the other, from merely social drinker to problem drinker, is usually imperceptible. So none of us can afford to be complacent about alcohol problems; any one of us may slip without knowing it from social into compulsive drinking – a transition which Elizabeth graphically described to us from her own experience.

Elizabeth's Story

Elizabeth cannot say at what point she became what the world calls an alcoholic. There was no *moment* up to which she had kept to the straight and narrow path, and after which she found herself fallen by the wayside. And yet she describes her adult life like some dark odyssey 'from social drinking, literally only at office parties, to a bottle of scotch a day'.

She found alcohol immediately attractive when she first tried it at the age of eighteen or nineteen. She had been a shy, introverted teenager and alcohol helped her lose the handicapping gaucheness which made all parties an agony. Then, in the nervousness of a first job, she found that a drink or two at lunch would release in her a much more confident and (she believed) competent office worker than she was otherwise. By this stage, alcohol was becoming an accessory to her work and her social life, but not until she had passed the age of twenty-five did it begin to become indispensable.

By her early thirties Elizabeth was a married woman, worked for one of the largest hotel chains in the world and always took her morning coffee laced with vodka. Yet she had an iron drinker's constitution – never had a hangover and could drink any man under the table. Once, after a bout of pneumonia, a doctor warned her she was an 'incipient alcoholic', but she took no notice. 'It seems to me now I just lacked all moral fibre', she says. 'If I wanted a drink I just had one.' Her unconcern was apparent rather than real. The marriage was under increasing strain, and at work she was beginning to uncover horrendous bungles which only she could have made, but of which she had no recollection. At this point she attempted suicide, was rushed into hospital, and spent a short time on a psychiatric ward. But no sooner was she was released than Elizabeth resumed her drinking as before.

When her husband was diagnosed as having cancer, she tried to give up drink in a real attempt to care for him. 'But after a while I suppose I got jealous of all the attention he was getting.' Another suicide attempt and another spell in hospital followed.

Elizabeth's husband died when she was forty. She had given

up her job three months earlier to nurse him, and now she simply stayed at home and drank. She had palpitations and sweats, but convinced herself these were something to do with the menopause, though she was too young for this. By the time she saw a doctor and began the long haul to sobriety, Elizabeth was, she thinks, in a pitiable state. 'I couldn't function without alcohol. I couldn't go out of the door to do the shopping without having a drink.'

Is Compulsive Drinking a Disease?

Bout drinkers such as Dylan Thomas and the chronically drunk like Elizabeth are two extremes of the condition known to most people as 'alcoholism'. The separation between these people and ordinary recreational drinkers seems so obvious that the alcoholic in recent years has come to be regarded as suffering from a *disease*, a physical or psychological disorder which marks them and sets them apart. This view of compulsive drinkers holds that while, for the majority, alcohol use is controllable, for an unfortunate few use inevitably become abuse, alcohol becomes the object of abnormal craving and an agent of addiction. Whatever the causes of this might be, they are regarded as the same kind of factors which cause all other diseases – probably genetic, possibly environmental influences over which the sufferer has no control, and which make him or her *constitutionally* different from the herd.

This is the view of alcoholism which you will find in Alcoholics Anonymous. AA members are taught that the course of the disease invariably flows through the same pattern, a slide down to 'rock bottom' followed by an upward curve to complete sobriety and life without alcohol. Recovery depends first on the recognition that one is in the grip of a disease for which there is no cure and over which one has no control and second that even a single drink smashes the recovery process, which must then be attempted from the beginning. This approach explains why AA members are required to identify themselves with the sentence *I am an alcoholic*. That self-definition is immutable. It defines their life and the course of action they must take to avoid self-destruction.

The AA method has certainly caught the imagination, for it is as powerful and dramatic as the revivalist evangelism from which it originally drew its inspiration. Also, and in spite of this history, AA is morally a more neutral approach than the old church-based temperance movements, which had viewed alcohol as 'sinful' rather than 'sick'. Yet in spite of its attractions, the explanation for problem drinking on which AA depends, and which was once the orthodox psychiatric theory, is now increasingly coming into question.

The most damaging evidence against the idea that there is a disease called alcoholism began to build up from a day in 1958 when a chance conversation at the Maudsley Hospital in London alerted one of the psychiatrists to the fact that several of their ex-alcoholic patients had resumed normal controlled drinking. On the old disease theory, this should have been impossible. That doctor, Dr D. L. Davies, then began a research project and found that out of ninety-four ex-patients, seven had been drinking normally five years after diagnosis and treatment for alcohol addiction. His findings outraged psychiatrists, since it seemed to undermine the basis of their conventional treatment of alcoholism – which rested on the idea that this was an incurable disease, for which the only answer was complete, life-long abstention. Yet the possibility of harm-free drinking in former alcoholics has since been confirmed by a large body of research during the the twenty years since Davies published his controversial results. If not yet completely demolished, the idea of an alcoholic disease nowadays is clinically much less secure.

As we shall see later this does not mean that all reformed problem drinkers should resume social drinking at once. For the moment we want to show that, once the disease theory begins to dissolve, the distinctions between compulsive drinking and 'normal' drinking become less compelling. Then the focus of attention shifts to the idea that there are degrees and differences between problem drinkers, and that these differences – between for instance the bout-boozer and the chronic 'drip-feed' drinker – become relatively more interesting. But we are running ahead of ourselves. We have talked a good deal about normal drinking, without giving very much idea of what this is.

A Thumbnail History of Drinking Norms

Drinking alcohol is not necessary and not particularly natural. Of course, fruits do ferment by themselves if left alone, and this must have led to the primitive discovery of ciders and wines. But unlike eating, there is nothing primal about the act of becoming intoxicated.

It should also be remembered that drunkenness is no modern evil. The fall of the Roman Empire has been attributed to vast over-consumption of wine, though, to be fair, this may be due partly to the Roman practice of adding lead during wine-making to sweeten the taste and reduce acidity. In Britain today we still drink less than half per head than was consumed at the highest peak of drinking in our history – the early eighteenth century. At that time there were three different classes of alcoholic drink, to suit the tastes and purses of three classes of the population. Gin had recently been introduced, and provided the desperate and degraded urban poor with the cheapest possible ticket to oblivion. The signs over the doors of the gin shops did not mince their words: 'Drunk for a penny; dead drunk for twopence; clean straw provided.' Meanwhile enormous quantities of beer were being consumed all over the country by peasants, for whom this dark, rich and alcoholically very strong beverage was not only an escape from dung and deprivation, but a necessary source of vitamins, minerals and calories. Finally wine, mostly port, was drunk by the more prosperous classes. Excess was the rule rather than the exception here – men habitually drank three or four bottles a day. A possible record was established by a Dr John Campbell, who drank thirteen bottles at a single sitting.

It has been estimated that, during this eighteenth-century peak of alcohol consumption, an average of 46 grammes per day were consumed for each member of the population. From that peak, drinking habits slowly declined until they reached the lowest trough during the austerity years after the Second World War, when only 8 grammes per day were consumed. These two figures provide the historical reference points by which we can judge our contemporary consumption, which is around 20 grammes per person per day.

In spite of the fact that this is up from an historically low figure, the rise is remarkable. Since 1700 there have only been two other periods when drinking increased, and neither occasion saw a large rise sustain itself for so long. What has caused this increase?

What Has Caused the Drinking Boom?

With the effects of economic recession still very much with us, many might think unemployment and poverty have had something to do with recent increases in drinking. Nothing is further from the truth. The great bulk of the increase is to do with our *prosperity* as a society increasing relative to the *price* and *availability* of alcohol. This equation has probably always been the most influential factor. In 1880 a London policeman told the social investigator William Booth that 'a great amount of drunkenness is still a sure sign of work being plentiful. It is then that the police are busiest.'

But no amount of plentiful work will lift the consumption of alcohol if the price of the stuff is rising faster than the cost of living. Over the past 250 years, whenever drink prices have risen sharply, overall national consumption has fallen almost as steeply. The effect was noted as early as 1690, when excise duty affecting beer was tripled from sixpence to one shilling and sixpence a pint. Consumption fell at once by about a third. In 1791, the tripling of duty on the malt used in brewing meant that 25 per cent less beer was drunk in the years following.

But these effects are only to do with *falls* in drinking. Does the trick work the other way? We have seen that, other than our own, there have been just two periods of increased alcohol drinking since 1700. Both were certainly caused by the introduction of cheaper liquor – cheap gin in the 1710s resulted in a 10 to 15 per cent increase, while the deregulation of brewing, which caused a sudden drop in beer prices in the 1880s, resulted in an extra pint being drunk each day for every man, woman and child of the population. The Saturday night problem of William Booth's policeman was only partly exacerbated by more plentiful work.

There is one other factor which regulates drinking, and that is the extent of its social approval. The steady decline in drinking through most of the nineteenth and twentieth centuries can partly be explained by the rising social aspirations and increasing sense of 'respectability' among the working class, alongside religious influences such as Methodism and, not least, the very influential temperance movement. Campaigns against drink have been a feature of our national life ever since the beginning of the Victorian age, and often had considerable popular success, which has not proved durable. In Ireland, for example, the Victorian temperance evangelist Father Mathew is said to have been personally responsible for a 22 per cent fall in drinking. Yet after his death, the deficit was speedily wiped out.

History, then, points to three reasons for the increase in drinking in Britain since 1950.

- The population as a whole has become increasingly prosperous.

- Excise duty has not kept pace with this prosperity – if it had, a bottle of Scotch whisky would today cost well over twenty pounds!

- Social disapproval has significantly waned, as churches and temperance movements have lost their influence and alcohol has shed its unrespectable image.

Drinking

The contemporary increase in drinking, which is proportionately a great deal larger than anything seen before, is therefore as much about relative price changes as about social change. Social permissiveness may have been a part of it, but public policy – the action (or inaction) of legislators in letting the real cost of liquor fall – must bear a larger share of the responsibility.

The Alcohol Problem

Where do problem drinkers like Elizabeth fit into this history? Can we say that they are any part of it? Certainly a rise of average daily alcohol intake to just over 20 grammes does not look so serious when compared with eighteenth-century rates of nearly 50 grammes. And why should an increase in average drinking – most of us, after all, would see ourselves as perfectly 'average' drinkers – lead to a rise in problem drinking?

At the same time, the effect of price rises in bringing alcohol consumption *down* also suggests that the effect is on controlled and reasonable drinking rather than the compulsive kind. The compulsive drinker might be expected to sacrifice some other commodity in order to maintain a continued supply of drink, while consumers who are free to choose will adjust their drinking in line with their means. This is what seemed to happen for a short period between 1979 and 1982, when a real but temporary increase in the cost of drink led consumption to fall for that period by 11 per cent, before resuming its overall increase after 1983.

However, some statisticians believe it is possible to predict the number of people in any society with a drinking problem simply by knowing the average consumption. Their graph means that for every rise and fall in average consumption there will be a consequent and inevitable fluctuation in alcoholism.

The experience of the past few years seems to bear this out, because problem drinking is almost certainly increasing rapidly in Britain. In 1950, hospital admissions of patients diagnosed as alcoholic numbered only 512. We have seen this figure increase by more than 25 times since then – partly but not entirely due to changes in diagnostic practice. Deaths from cirrhosis of the liver have doubled in the same period, a similar or slightly greater increase has been recorded for other alcohol-related diseases, as well as for drink-driving offences and convictions in the courts for simple drunkenness. One final indication of how awareness of this problem is increasing: in the last decade membership of Alcoholics

Anonymous has shot up from 13,400 to more than 35,000 – an increase of 161 per cent.

We have now reached the nub of the drink problem. On the one hand we have distinguished between normal or average drinking, which is under reasonable control, and compulsive drinking, which is not. On the other hand, we have suggested some link between compulsive drinking and reasonable drinking. Clearly the relationship between the two needs to be looked at more closely.

What is Normal Drinking?

On the face of it, normal non-problematic drinking seems easy to distinguish from problem drinking. The most obvious method is to set a threshold to the amount consumed, and call anything over and above that limit 'problem drinking'. The threshold has been set at various levels by doctors and health educators. Amounts of alcohol are measured in 'units', so that one unit is one half pint of standard beer, one to two glasses of wine or one measure of spirits. In the 1960s the daily allowance used to be put at sixteen units a day, at least eight pints of beer – beyond that the drinker was at risk from serious physical illness and/or addiction. Today most experts agree that this figure been should be put much lower, but the suggested levels vary a good deal.

In 1984 the Research Committee of the Royal College of Psychiatrists put the safe limit at nine units a day. In the same year Dr Ian Robertson, a leading psychologist who studies drinking, published an article in the *British Medical Journal* in which he said the safe limit for men was 'six or seven units'. Only two years later, in his book *Let's Drink To Your Health*, Dr Robertson had revised his own threshold down to no more than *five* units a day – that is, only two and a half pints of beer. The charity Alcohol Concern also says five units is the threshold. We have even seen *four* units quoted as an upper threshold. It must be remembered that these are safe limits for *men*. Women's bodies have a higher ratio of fat (which does not absorb alcohol) to fluid (which does) and this means alcohol is 'spread more thickly' in women. Therefore women's safety levels are between a third and a half lower than men's, only thirteen units a *week*. Of course it would be very unsafe to drink the week's allowance in one sitting, and most doctors advise pregnant women not to drink alcohol at all.

So if medical estimates of what are normally safe *quantities* of alcohol are not in complete agreement, perhaps we can find the essence of problem drinking not in how much people drink, but in their reasons for drinking, and the style in which they do it.

Three apparently secure criteria of normal drinking have been suggested. These are that first, normal drinkers know why they drink; second, they do so out of free and reasonable choice; and third, they treat drinking as a non-essential luxury, rather than a necessity upon which other activities depend.

Yet even these seemingly obvious statements fall down when you start to think more deeply about 'normal' drinking. All of the following would regard themselves as falling well outside the net of problem drinking, and – much more importantly – so would their friends and neighbours.

(1) He reckons the last works outing was a complete disaster 'because we ran out of drink before anyone could get comatose.'

(2) If she goes out for a meal, she avoids Chinese and Indian restaurants because 'I do like to have wine, and it doesn't go with oriental food.'

(3) He simply 'can't even imagine' sitting in a pub without an alcoholic drink.

(4) She hates the taste of alcohol, yet she always drinks when she goes out with her boyfriend, because 'he expects it. I have Rum and Coke because with that you only really taste the Coke.'

(5) Every day at half past six he gets home from the office. The first thing he does is pour himself a Scotch. If there is no Scotch in the house he buys a bottle on the way home.

(6) She never used to buy alcohol for the home until her supermarket started stocking an attractively displayed range of wines. Now she finds she never goes through the check-out without a couple of bottles.

(7) He is part of a round-buying circle. So when he goes to the pub he knows he is in for a minimum of six pints, like it or not.

(8) At nineteen she was up for a job, and her friend told her to have a stiff vodka half an hour before the interview. She got the job,

and now 'wouldn't dream of going for an interview without having a drink first'.

(9)   He is twenty-six. For a decade he has gone to football or cricket matches every week, carrying two four-packs of the strongest available lager. He says, 'only wimps go in with less'.

(10) She 'can't face the thought of sex unless I'm a bit tipsy'.

Of these cases, numbers three, five and six do not know why they feel or behave as they do; numbers three to seven cannot be said to exercise free and deliberate choice in all their drinking; and in every case (except, perhaps, number six), alcohol is regarded not as a luxury, but as necessary to at least one activity.

The truth is that alcohol has many uses other than giving the drinker a buzz. Many of these are to do with the way alcohol has become integrated into our social lives. Drinking does not merely make you more sociable by taking away your inhibitions, it makes you more socially acceptable to many groups of people, especially to teenagers and young adults, and most especially to young men. In one survey published by the government in 1985 no less than 35 per cent of young men with jobs described themselves as 'heavy drinkers'. Most of them would undoubtedly have been quite proud of this, since drinking together is often a symbol of group solidarity. Drunken exploits are important topics of male conversation in which an ability to hold your drink is held up as a sign of maturity, strength and virility.

In our society young men are expected to bear few responsibilities, and their drinking behaviour may be simply a consequence of this – what you might call a passing phase. If so, once they marry and acquire responsibilities, these attitudes ought to fall away. And so they do – but not very much. The same survey found that, of working males in the age range twenty-five to forty-five, 28 per cent *still* claimed to be heavy drinkers. For such men the cult of alcohol has maintained its hold, either as a continuation of their earliest drinking behaviour, or perhaps in the more burdensome form of a real drink problem.

As soon as drink acquires a significant meaning beyond itself, then elements of compulsion begin to creep in. Where it is a powerful index of enjoyment, for instance, or the success of a social occasion, then people who give parties will try to maximise the amounts consumed – they will press their guests to have more than they would otherwise have. Where it is a symbol of virility, feats of drinking will be attempted as trials of strength.

Learning to Drink

What we have said about normal drinking shows that drinking – even more than eating – means little outside its context, but a great deal when you see how and why people learn to do it. But how important is this element of learning to drink in the genesis of the compulsive drinker?

Peter's Story

Peter is a 38-year-old surveyor who reckons he has spent twenty-three years of his life drinking. He told us: 'Neither of my parents were drinkers. My father was a musician and as a result we saw little of him as kids. When I was ten or eleven I remember my mother leaving home for a short time – although I don't blame her for leaving, you do feel a sense of rejection and that period was hell for my younger sister and myself. I became very confused and fed up with life ... in fact for as long as I remember I've always been a funny kid and very mixed up inside.'

Peter started drinking when taking his school exams, meeting a couple of friends in the pub and drinking with that group regularly, three pints each, a round apiece. But Peter found that the drink made him feel even more mixed up. Yet although he did not really like it, and it got him into trouble several times, he persisted with it. His studies prospered and he eventually took his degree, but he found himself unable to take any of this seriously. 'You put up a complete front, as society wants from you, although you feel pissed off inside. I had absolutely no confidence in myself.'

Peter became quickly disillusioned with his first job as a draughtsman – 'I drank my way through most of that.' He married at twenty-five, straight from home, and now has an eleven-year-old daughter, but the marriage lasted only three years. When he thinks about his daughter, whom he sees just once a fortnight, he is 'sad that I may have upset her life, but I feel that I must act like a responsible adult when I'm in her company'.

So far we have seen that Peter feels badly about the course of his life. What did his problems amount to? He has a sense of having been rejected by parents who in his childhood were often absent or

37

falling out with each other. Following on from this, there was a more than usually confused adolescence, lack of belief in himself, inability to take his work seriously, a broken marriage and guilt about the effect of this on his young daughter. On top of it all, he drank too much from an early age, even though he did not really like it.

We might ask why drink? The first and obvious explanation is that drink provided anaesthesia for the unhappiness he felt inside. But that is not reason enough, since as he tells us, he did not *like* drinking. He began drinking *not* because he was unhappy, but because that is what young men do. They learn to do it by imitating and emulating their friends. It was not until Peter discovered that drink could not only give him a context for his social life, but provide him also with an *excuse* to act out the part he had created for himself, that his drink 'problem' began.

Peter is capable, even talented at his job, but drink makes him 'purposefully destroy what I'd achieved'. He loves his family, yet drink destroyed his marriage. As he says: 'I was on a destruction course, and I was scared stiff of life. I used drink as a crutch, and the crutch was screwing up my life.'

The movement from normal to problem drinking can be seen in Peter's story. Two elements in particular illustrate our explanation of compulsions. First, Peter, like the compulsive eaters in the previous chapter, had many unresolved emotions about his family and his own personality; and second, he learned to drink (though not to enjoy it) and then to adapt the drinking habit into both a crutch and a weapon against himself. So Peter ended up quite deliberately using drink as a method of coping with his primary problems, in such a way that this became for him a *compulsory* method of coping.

We spoke to several people who had slipped from social to compulsive drinking when they were trying to deal with a life crisis, and who found that the crutch of alcohol quickly became a lash, as it did for Alan.

Alan's Story

Alan, a northerner in his fifties, had worked in the travel business for thirty years and 'everyone drinks in travel'. He was a regular pub drinker and his social life centred around drinking with his darts team. Unexpectedly he was faced with redundancy and took early retirement at fifty-five. The shock and anxiety of this, and the loneliness he felt, made him turn to the bottle. His regular drinking was now supplemented by whisky throughout the day. When he could not sleep, he found himself taking a drink at six in the morning.

After six months, during which he also faced eviction from his flat, he woke up one morning covered in blood from a fall he could not remember. A friend took him to hospital, where his drink problem was recognised. The shock of that stay in hospital made him vow never to drink spirits again. For the past eighteen months he has stuck to this, and although still a regular social drinker, he knows he must be on his guard against backsliding into his previous compulsive drinking pattern.

Some people would contrast Alan and Peter by saying that Peter was an 'addict' while Alan – since he was able to give up spirits while continuing to take alcohol – was not. In fact, the difference between patterns of drinking are never so clear cut. However there are some points to be made about the physical aspects of alcohol dependence.

Addiction

Alcohol is certainly a psychologically addictive (or compulsive) drug, with all the consequences of that. It is also, however, physically addictive, in that the body does build up tolerance to it. Elizabeth's daily intake was considerable, but she was able to work more or less normally and not appear incapacitated. It is said that the comedian and notorious alcoholic W. C. Fields, when young, was well able to combine a daily schedule of six performances of a complicated juggling act with a gin habit of a quart-and-a-half a day. His body compensated and coped – though the long-term consequences of his drinking were less happy.

Physical addiction's most tell-tale signs are the withdrawal symptoms, and these are widely thought to be the same thing as *delirium tremens* (DTs). However DTs are in fact the extreme manifestation of withdrawal. Fearful hallucinations are conjured out of previously damped-down brain cells which – in the absence of the normal level of alcohol – have become over-excited. But every drinker who has ever had a hangover has known some of the more minor withdrawal symptoms.

Physical addiction is not the test of alcoholism (or of the *alcohol dependence syndrome*, as it is usually called today). You can be a problem drinker without ever experiencing withdrawal – Elizabeth told us she had never had a hangover until she'd been a compulsive drinker for years. Nevertheless, addiction is one of the most serious end-points of the compulsive drinker's behaviour, a goal towards which it tends, perhaps over one or two decades, before it is a reality, perhaps never quite becoming so. However, for many compulsives, it is not until this extreme point has been reached that the compulsive drinker scrapes against the 'rock bottom' of degradation without which, according to Alcoholics Anonymous, a full recovery cannot be ensured.

So What is a Problem Drinker?

We have seen how the difference between normal and problem drinking can be hard to make out. At its simplest, of course, the difference is in the word 'problem', and drinkers' problems nearly always come out in their relationships with others.

It is probably useless to ask the individual drinker 'do you have a problem with drink?' Problem drinkers always know they have a difficulty, but they usually cannot acknowledge that drink is part of it. Alcohol for them is the *answer* - not a very good one, perhaps, but it 'gets them through'. Their extreme drinking behaviour then appears as a mask, hiding their true problem(s) – partly from themselves but, even more importantly, from other people.

But, just like the eating disorders of the last chapter, there is also the self-destructive aspect of the compulsion, the lash. Often those close to a person put up stiff resistance to the idea that their friend or loved one has a drink problem. But when they see what the heavy drinker is doing to him or herself, the scales drop from their eyes and at last they see someone who is dependent on alcohol. It is the lash of problem drinking rather than the mask which alerts the drinker's family and colleagues to the need for action.

So the first stage in the process of getting help is not necessarily at the drinker's own command: it may depend on the responses of those nearby, and whether they can see behind the mask of compulsive behaviour. The next stage, however, is even more uncertain than this – the drinker's own acceptance that help is needed.

Steve's Story

Steve had his first alcoholic drink as a very small baby, when his mother used to give him teaspoons of whisky to make him sleep. As a child he was disturbed, and had psychiatric treatment for emotional disturbance: his parents, he says, cared for him poorly and starved him of affection.

As a boy chorister he discovered altar wine, and would resort to this in times of stress. By the age of fourteen he had graduated to other drinks, not in great quantities, but regularly and usually alone. After school Steve had a spell in a psychiatric hospital, where for the first time he felt safe and secure. Then he found work and, like Elizabeth's, this was a job which gave him unlimited access to alcohol, for it was in the wine and spirit trade. For ten years he worked his way up to be Personnel Manager – somewhat ironic in view of his chronic inability to form satisfactory relationships with any person. There followed a suicide attempt, redundancy, a new job, storms over his drinking, resignation and four years of 'rock bottom' living 'in the gutter'. His family would have nothing to do with him. The hospital constantly dried him out, but he never stayed sober for long. Steve was still quite unable to foresee life without alcohol.

Though he ended up in a heap, Steve found the will to survive. Alcoholics Anonymous provided him with the platform from which to relaunch his life on a new basis, not 'suffocated' by alcohol and able to build a more positive self-image. At forty-two Steve has not had a drink now for seven years.

Getting Well: the AA Approach

There is no doubt that AA is successful in helping many people. It works through groups of members meeting together in the solidarity of a common identity ('I am an alcoholic'), offering mutual understanding in the struggle with what is perceived as a disease you are born with. The AA group is a place with no illusions – at least none of the kind which once led its members into drinking. Each member knows where they all stand, knows what they are trying to do ('stay sober one day at a time') and knows the penalties for failure (a 'spiral back down to rock bottom'). For a great many people this approach has been of proven worth.

But some of AA's strengths must also be counted among its weaknesses. Its authoritarianism, and the puritanical, evangelical strain out of which it sprang, are enough to alienate many – especially the young. In an age when drinking problems among youth are surging, this is on its own cause to seek alternative approaches.

Compulsion

Medical Approaches

Unlike AA, which says there is no treatment for alcoholism except the defensive avoidance of the poison of alcohol, doctors use hospital care and psychotherapy, first to remove the physical effects of drinking (and then of giving up drink), and then to try to deal with the life problems of the patient. Some of these are frankly behaviourist methods, identifying the problems as by and large about the drinking behaviour itself. The most patent 'cure' is Antabuse, a drug which, if you drink on top of it, makes you violently ill with nausea, vomiting and stomach cramps. This can be implanted, so that the treatment continues beyond the hospital and into 'normal life'. Antabuse is a frank attempt to cure the patient by coercion – to *force* a life without drink. A few people may be helped by it, but as we saw with eating disorders, such approaches may be counter-productive. After all, is it appropriate to use 'punishments' with people who are already, as often as not, punishing themselves? Steve had Antabuse implants but they merely made him more desperate, degraded and uncontrolled.

AA is more likely to have success than punishment-and-reward regimes, because it returns the onus, at least for future behaviour, to the individual, while Antabuse is there to be fought against. Behavioural treatment in a good clinic would not, in any case, be tried on its own. The priority, according to Dr Ian Robertson of the Astley Ainsley Hospital in Edinburgh, must be to try to understand the nature of the drinking problem. One helpful first step is to keep a drinking diary, similar to the log of eating habits kept by the compulsive eater or dieter. To know your pattern of drinking, and what you associate it with, is vital in gaining insight.

Dr Robertson is conscious of how difficult it really is to see where the 'normal' compulsions around social drinking (such as we have described above) become abnormal, destructive behaviour. He emphasises how different and how individual all drinking problems are, though there are regularities of a kind which are found in many other compulsions – secretiveness, emotional blackmail, self-pity, the tendency to manipulate people, the preoccupation with the compulsion to the exclusion of everything else.

The mask and the lash each play their parts – in varying degrees – from one compulsive person to the next, and these need to be understood. Steve spoke of being 'suffocated' by drink – as if by a mask that was too tight. Peter felt he was like a cripple beating himself with his own stick. Elizabeth 'couldn't go out of the door' without putting on the mask of a quick drink.

The variability of these states is one of the most important things about them. Sometimes drinking problems resolve themselves on their own. On the other hand, they sometimes lead on a downward spiral to an apparently inevitable early death. If the therapist and the drinker can understand the singularity of the drinking be-haviour, this gives clues to the life changes which must be made in order to overcome the problem. Dr Robertson reminds us that not *all* problem drinkers need to foreswear all alcohol for ever. Controlled drinking is possible – though he stresses that many – even most – problem drinkers do better in the long run if they can give up all drink. Anyone who has already dealt with their drinking problem with abstinence, or who has suffered physical harm from abusing drink (such as a heart complaint or liver damage) should under no circumstances attempt to return to controlled drinking.

Reaching the Primary Problem

Before there is hope of a real solution to alcohol compulsion, an alleviation of the primary problem must have occurred. AA does this by offering drinkers the kind of closeness, warmth and 'uplift' which has usually been so conspicuously lacking in their lives. There are of course other ways of achieving this. A change for the better in one's emotional life might do it – a new job, a move to another environment, a marriage. It is remarkable how many alcoholics tell a tale of emotional deprivation in childhood. Of the cases discussed in this chapter, Elizabeth, Steve and Peter all had upbringings of this kind.

Prevention

It is not within the power of governments to make people love their children, although social conditions in which parents – especially young parents – bring up their families and the educational back-up they receive are crucial. We will return to this theme in the context of mental health in general in the last chapter. For the moment, and just to speak of alcohol, it is clear that government has been progressively less interested in controlling alcohol consumption in the post-war years. Government revenues from alcohol sales are now at about two billion pounds, and perhaps the Exchequer fears a falling-off of revenue if consumption drops following a rise in duties. Yet in fact we have seen two budgets running, 1986 and 1987, when excise duty on alcohol has not risen at all, not even by levels to match inflation. As a result the price of drink has continued to fall in real terms.

In this chapter we have argued that alcohol abuse has its roots in alcohol use. More specifically, we have seen how the general *cost* of alcohol determines not only the level of normal drinking, but also the amounts of compulsive drinking. Some people will drink compulsively at whatever level they can afford. But if drink is expensive they will consume relatively *less* than otherwise, and there will be a relative reduction in physical damage. Others, however, if they cannot afford so many visits to the pub and the off-licence, may never fall into the problem drinking trap in the first place.

It was estimated in 1985 that the two billion pounds revenue accrued by the state from alcohol was completely cancelled out by the cost of treating the totality of alcohol-related diseases by the health services, which is also put at two billion pounds. This in itself is a remarkable coincidence. But two years on, when medical costs have continued to rise at a rate higher than inflation, we have seen government alcohol revenues remain at this amount – i.e. they have fallen in real terms. So today, as a society, we are all net losers from alcohol-related problems. That situation makes no sense whatever.

Many of the problems connected with alcohol consumption derive from its public availability and wide public acceptance. Until these two factors change, there seems no reason why there should not be increasing numbers of drinkers who will use the alcohol compulsion as a way of coping with their emotional and other problems.

Chapter 3

Taking Tranquilliser

*... there was an impudent mountebank who sold pills
which (he told the country people) were very good
against earthquakes. Joseph Addison*

Twenty years ago the Rolling Stones recorded a song called
'Mother's Little Helper', a rock 'n roll anthem of doomed old age:
'what a drag it is getting old.' The Helper of the title is a 'little yellow
pill', a tranquilliser of a kind which – in the 1960s – was a marvellous
new invention, a supposedly non-addictive and benign substitute for
the old, highly dangerous tranquillisers of the barbiturate group.
These new safe drugs were technically called the *benzodiazapines* but
many of them soon became household names under their trade titles:
Librium, Mogadon, Ativan and, most famous of all, Valium.

The Stones' song was quite lacking in compassion for the
members of the mother-generation who went 'running for the
shelter' of such drugs. The pills, of course, had none of the glamour
associated at that time with marijuana, Purple Heart 'uppers' and
mind-expanding LSD. However, in spite of the caustic tones of the
record, it was slightly ahead of its time in two ways. First, it rightly
identified this as a drug of dependence, which most doctors would
then have denied. Second, it explicitly linked the use of the drug
with the existence of serious life problems – loneliness, fear of
growing old, depression, insomnia, alienation.

What are Tranquillisers?

The so-called 'major tranquillisers', such as Largactil
(chlorpromazine), are used for treating serious psychotic diseases,
and it is not these we are concerned with here. The tranquillising
drugs in most common use today are the 'minor tranquillisers', most
of which are in fact benzodiazapines. These drugs were introduced
in the early 1960s in response to growing fears over the dangers of
barbiturates, which were then widely used in hundreds of prepara-

tions, but which have strong intoxicating and addictive qualities and are very easy to overdose. The new benzodiazapines were brought in as the 'safe' alternative.

Like barbiturates, benzodiazapines are 'downers'. Their effect is very similar to alcohol in that they suppress brain function. The benzodiazapine compounds themselves were discovered in 1933, but it was not until the early 1960s that they were found to have a taming effect on wild animals. When tried in humans, four useful medical functions were identified for these drugs. They calm general brain activity down (sedation), they are effective in reducing worry (anti-anxiety), they release spasm in muscles (muscle-relaxant) and they stop fits and seizures (anti-convulsant).

The anti-anxiety effect of these drugs was widely seized on at the popular end of medical journalism, and they began to be called Happiness Pills. Humanity has a recurring fantasy that one day such a magic pill will appear. Aldous Huxley described it in *Brave New World*, and called it *soma*. In *Brave New World Revisited*, the author summarised the advantages of *soma* as follows: 'In small doses it brought a sense of bliss, in larger doses it made you see visions and, if you took three tablets, you would sink in a few minutes into refreshing sleep. And all at no physiological or mental cost. The Brave New Worlders could take holidays from their black moods, or from the familiar annoyances of everyday life, without sacrificing their health or permanently reducing their efficiency.' In short, this was the perfect tranquilliser, and the scientists who synthesised the benzodiazapines in the early 1960s thought they had discovered *soma* in real life.

Many drugs – alcohol, opium, heroin, LSD, cannabis, nicotine, thalidomide, even coffee – had been previously cast in this role only, in the end, to be found wanting, usually because of side-effects, the 'kick in the tail'.

Only potions in fantasy fiction have no side-effects. At first those attached to the benzodiazapines were regarded as fairly unimportant. They can, for example, interfere with certain everyday activities significantly, but not catastrophically. Driving and the operation of machines is impaired, and the drugs produce a dragging sense of lethargy, a lack of concentration and perhaps confusion. Sometimes they bring about exaggerated excitement and intoxication, similar to alcohol, whose effects they can increase if the two are taken together. And like alcohol, they can leave you with a hangover. A final consideration is that most of these are long-lasting drugs, though the length of their effect depends on the type used.

Some persist in the body for up to thirty-six hours. This means that there can be cumulative effects if the interval between doses is reduced.

Yet the *soma*-like image of Valium and the other benzodiazapines was not completely destroyed by these unwanted effects. Sensible use, it was felt, would avoid them, and, for doctors, there were tremendous medical advantages. Apart from the sheer convenience of being able to prescribe a drug which quelled a patient's anxiety and distress, benzodiazapine is difficult to overdose, does not (like barbiturate) damage the liver, is very easily absorbed and takes effect quickly. Above all, nobody thought it was addictive. The 'miracle-drug' aura which surrounded these new tranquillisers when they first appeared, and which is still promoted by seductive drug company advertising, is echoed in many of their commercial brand-names: Librium, Valrelease, Evacalm, Serenid and (our favourite) Halcion. The last name, in particular, seems almost an obscene travesty of what these pills can do, as Tina's tragic experience shows.

Tina's Story

Tina Peters is forty now. She believes benzodiazapine tranquillisers are responsible for depriving her of half her life.

Tina was pregnant and nineteen when she was given her first tranquillisers – for symptoms of nausea. She was not told at the time, but her prescription was for a barbiturate. She had another spell on this same drug during her next pregnancy two and a half years later. Then, when Tina's second daughter was born, she had severe post-natal depression combined with serious marital difficulties. Her doctor prescribed Librium and referred her to a psychiatrist. Tina believed they thought she was going mad.

The psychotherapy was unsuccessful – partly because the doctor lost patience when Tina's husband proved withdrawn and uncommunicative. Tina simply continued to take her Librium, seeing three different doctors over the next two years, with none of them raising an eyebrow. When a fourth general practitioner suggested that she switch from 10-microgramme to 5-microgramme tablets she panicked in case this was not enough. However when she contacted one of the other doctors he told her to 'just take two tablets instead of one'.

By now Tina was heavily dependent on the drug, but would not acknowledge it. She twice tried to come off the pills on her own.

For two days she would feel wonderful, with a sense of freedom. 'But on the third day I was just climbing up the walls. I felt demented, terrible, insane. My brain just wouldn't function properly, apart from feeling agoraphobic, claustrophobic, paranoia, all sorts of awful mental conditions. It's been a nightmare, I've been to hell and back.'

During the whole period of her daughter Sarah's growing up, Tina was unknowingly a tranquilliser addict. Sarah told us that she and her sister realised this, but discussed it with no one. Their mother's response to the tranquilliser seemed paradoxical. She was obsessively preoccupied with housework, and with constant activity. She never even had time to read the papers, but was adamant that they should not be thrown away until she *had* read them. So newspapers would pile up for weeks on end in the house. She would never relax; she thought she had no time to sit down to eat, she was too busy even to cook sometimes. Her temper was always on a short fuse. Sarah does not think her mother ever saw the tranquillisers as a problem: the problem, she thought, was in her, and the pills were essential to 'keep her going.'

Tina, of course, was not alone. As we shall see later, millions of people have been affected by the twenty-year fashion for prescribing these drugs, a fashion made possible by the public's illusions about the power of medicine, coupled with a straightforward but disastrous medical mistake: the benzodiazapines, it turned out, *did* cause dependence after all. So what exactly were the consequences of this?

Dependence

A change in medical language usually signals a new attitude towards the patient. In the history of alcohol-related medicine for instance, the shift from the Victorian term 'dipsomania' *via* 'alcoholism' to the modern concept of an 'alcohol dependence syndrome' has charted the growth of a more flexible view of the patient's condition.

Behind the emergence of the term *drug dependence*, as opposed to *addiction*, has been a similar change. The word 'addict' originally meant a 'devotee' – someone who chose to be bound to a habit or practice. 'Dependence' has a very much more passive and accidental ring to it.

Certainly this fits people like Tina, who seem to have been purely passive victims of a medical oversight. Such victims are not a new phenomenon, and these are not the worst of recent times:

thalidomide (another sedative) must be reckoned a worse, though less widespread, disaster. Nevertheless the psychological toll of the minor tranquillisers *is* a disaster for their victims, and a gross miscarriage of medical and natural justice.

The sense of unfairness comes because these are people who have put themselves trustingly in the hands of medicine in the hope of alleviating their symptoms, in many cases symptoms which are patently caused by serious life problems – marriage difficulties, financial worries, etc. What they have received is just *another* problem: drug dependence. And here the *passivity* of the idea of drug dependence is highly appropriate, since the whole problem has been brought about not by their own choice, but by medical ignorance, if not negligence.

How does this fit our view of compulsions? After all, in the case of eating disorders and alcohol abuse we have seen the compulsion to be instigated very much by the individual sufferer. However, in two important respects, tranquilliser dependence comes about in very similar ways to the problem drinking and compulsive eating behaviour which we have looked at in previous chapters.

First, the existence of a primary problem is self-evident in tranquilliser compulsion, since the patient goes to the doctor with anxiety, insomnia or depression, all indications of more or less serious life problems. Second, the tranquilliser is prescribed as a method of *coping*: in fact, this is its only function, since it does not solve the life problems themselves. Initially it assists coping extremely well. As one user put it, 'Valium gives you a high. You don't think about things anymore, they don't matter. So you can swan through the day, sleep well at night and feel you're having a good time. You don't fall over or anything, I mean you're not an embarrassment. You just don't *worry* about anything – it's as simple as that.'

The Valium high sounds just like *soma*. But there is one significant difference. With Huxley's fictional tranquilliser 'the holiday it gave was perfect and, if the morning after was disagreeable, it was … only by comparison with the joys of the holiday. The remedy was to make the holiday continuous.' Wanting to apply this remedy is, of course, the compulsive side of all misused psychoactive drugs. But unfortunately, because of the inconvenient phenomenon of *tolerance*, the Valium holiday is not, and cannot be, continuous.

The physical effectiveness of a benzodiazapine tranquilliser is short-lived. Its ability to depress cell function (from which, like alcohol, its pleasant effects are derived) begins to waver after only a few days of continuous use, and it is now thought to become completely ineffective as an anti-anxiety medicine after four months. Its power over insomnia declines even faster – it becomes ineffective, if taken every night, after as little as two weeks. This falling away of the drug's effectiveness happens because the brain cells which it depresses begin to adapt, learning to work round the drug. That learning process is the biological meaning of tolerance.

We have already seen how tolerance happens with alcohol, resulting for instance in the experienced drinker taking much longer to get drunk than the inexperienced one. It happens even more dramatically, as we shall find later, with users of drugs derived from opium. In the case of any of these drugs, if you take them over a period and want to continue to experience physical effects at the same level, the *only way* to do so is to step up the dose.

There is also a phenomenon called *cross-tolerance* where one substance can build up tolerance on behalf of another. There is for instance a marked cross-tolerance effect between tranquillisers and alcohol. One hospital doctor told us that he once gave Valium to an alcoholic patient who was suffering from total amnesia, and was surprised to find him 'soaking it up like a sponge', until the dose was a massive 100 mg (the normal starting dose being only 2 mg). The patient's heavy alcohol consumption meant that a normal dose of the tranquilliser was completely ineffective.

In compulsive users of tranquillisers tolerance means that the original effects of the drug – the ones for which they were prescribed – dwindle and disappear. Then why do so many people, like Tina, go on taking the drug over years without craving an ever-increasing dose? There is a positive reason for this, and a negative one.

Psychological Dependence

We saw with alcohol that there are two categories of dependence, physical and psychological, and both apply to tranquillisers as much as to drinking. Psychological dependence partly involves mental conditioning, and in the case of tranquilliser use it is reinforced by medical approval. The doctor is not only an authority figure but the source of the tranquilliser prescriptions, so it is quite reasonable to suppose that 'if the doctor's giving it to me it must be doing some good'. Such beliefs are very powerful in medicine. They are allied to the 'placebo effect', whereby inactive preparations like chalk or sugar pills – if the patient believes in them – can be as good as the most powerful medicines. And, as we saw with eating compulsions, once a person with problems becomes psychologically convinced that some course of action (slimming or taking pills) is a *solution* to that problem, then they are spurred on compulsively to continue with that course of action. The final point to emphasise here is that the diminishing effect of tolerance does not operate in psychological dependence. Quite the reverse, in fact. The longer a psychologically-motivated compulsion is continued, the more deep-seated it becomes. Psychological dependence, then, is the positive reason why people go on taking a particular dose of tranquillisers, in spite of having built up a physical tolerance.

The negative reason is that it is simply too painful to give up.

Tranquillisers and Withdrawal

We have seen how, when Tina tried come off Librium, she was perfectly well for a couple of days (because it takes two days for many benzodiazapines to be eliminated from the body), but soon she was going 'up the wall'. Tina's withdrawal symptoms happened for the same reason that they do in alcohol dependence – her body was so completely used to the presence of the drug that it went haywire when deprived of it. In case anyone should think that sufferers exaggerate the discomfort of withdrawal (Tina went 'to hell and back') here is a list of symptoms which *may* accompany withdrawal: sleep disturbance, irritability, increased tension, anxiety, panic attacks, paranoid delusions, shaking, profuse sweating, poor concentration, visual disturbance, heightened sensitivity to sights, sounds, etc., depersonalisation, a sense of unreality, nausea, dry retching, epileptic seizures, weight loss, palpitations, muscular pains and stiffness.

Another sufferer, Christine, described her experiences to us as follows:

'It was the fright of going out, meeting people. Going out into the open. The sensation that you were going to collapse, you know ... Bright lights and noises. I couldn't stand traffic, I couldn't stand neon lights flashing or anything like that. And going into shops with bright lights. I'd push myself and make myself go and pay for something. But that panic was always there, I'd got to get out.'

This 'hell' might not be so bad if it were brief. Yet depending on the type of tranquilliser, it can take up to a month for the body to return to normal – a very long time indeed to live with a permanent craving for that one pill which you know will take away the pain instantaneously. It is probably easier to give up smoking, since

51

nicotine withdrawal symptoms only last three or four days.

These are the aspects of the tranquilliser compulsion itself, or at least the elements of the problem which are to do with the pills. But behind that problem lurk, as ever, other difficulties. It is these which, with the connivance of the medical profession, have led so many people into the tranquilliser trap. How did Christine, whose withdrawal symptoms we have quoted, find herself in that trap?

Christine's Story

It began when Christine was pregnant for the second time, close on the birth of her first baby. Then suddenly, her own mother died and Christine found herself running two homes – looking after her father and her four younger brothers and sisters, as well as her own. After six months of this she was 'on the verge of a breakdown' and she saw her doctor, who gave her a series of different tranquillisers before settling on Ativan as the one that 'did the trick'. Christine was then stabilised on a repeat prescription of two and a half milligrammes of Ativan three times a day for the next seventeen years. She never properly realised that she was dependent, although if she forgot to take the drug she experienced what she now knows to have been withdrawal symptoms.

During those seventeen years Christine was having constant symptoms – severe headaches, fearful depressions and attacks of agoraphobia, when she feared to go out of the house. She would wait for someone to pass by her door and ask them to do her shopping for her. Although she saw her doctor regularly (to renew her Ativan prescription), he never suggested any other treatment

It seems obvious to Christine now that she should never have been treated with tranquillisers in the first place. She believes that the primary cause of her near breakdown was the need to grieve for her mother, which she had suppressed in face of the demands of her family. Her doctor's well-meaning provision of a seventeen-year drug habit served to stifle that grief before she could express it, but she is sure that some kind of breakdown would have been preferable. When she finally broke the habit in a self-help group, the group leader was the first person in all those years who made a connection between the near breakdown (which led to the tranquilliser compulsion) and the death of Christine's mother. After several sessions with this perceptive woman, Christine was able to grieve for her mother for the first time.

Taking Tranquillisers

Christine had seen a television programme about tranquilliser dependence, and it dawned on her that she might be dependent on Ativan. She decided to give it up, although two doctors in her practice tried to dissuade her, and the third, while sympathetic, was cautious. She heard about the self-help project where she did an eight-week course in how to come off tranquillisers. This, with a sense of incredible relief, she eventually did. But the story has a postscript.

Eight weeks after she had taken her last pill, she visited her doctor with an unrelated problem. Their consultation was interrupted by a telephone call, and, when the doctor put down the phone, he referred absent-mindedly to her notes and said 'well, if we can't sort this out, I think we'll put you back on the Ativan.'

Christine could hardly believe her ears.

This Pill Culture

This doctor's pill-pushing reflex seems almost incredible in the context of Christine's life and her struggles to give up taking the drug. But against the background of medical practice generally, it is not such a surprise. Estimates of the number of tranquillisers being taken vary, but we do know that there are more than twenty million tranquilliser prescriptions filled out in Britain each year. Only five years ago, when warnings on dependence were placed on the label for the first time, that figure was thirty million.

Ron Lacey, director of the mental health charity MIND, indicts doctors and pharmaceutical companies as, to all intents and purposes, licensed drug-pushers. Certainly the prescribing of drugs is one of the holy rituals of seeing the doctor – up to 75 per cent of consultations with the family doctor end with a prescription, though this proportion is now beginning to fall.

A surprisingly large number of us are familiar with tranquillisers. One in five women and one in ten men take such a pill at least once in the course of a year, and more than a half of them are on a course of treatment lasting a month or more. It is now estimated that three million people are at risk from tranquilliser addiction.

Without the drug companies, the doctor would have nothing to prescribe. But should the source of therapeutic information be the same as the source of the drugs themselves? About 45 per cent of the doctor's information about *new* medicines comes from pharmaceutical companies.

A lot of hard sell is used to persuade doctors to prescribe drug products – not only free samples but inducements ranging from free calenders, thermometers and pens to research grants and travel to conferences abroad. A doctor's post-bag is phenomenal – the mail-shots from pharmaceutical companies to an average family doctor would fill a generous sized carrier-bag every two days. They cannot read everything, and it is certain that what information gets through is that presented in the slickest and most attention-grabbing style. But slickness is no guarantee of medical worth.

There are other pressures which condition doctors into reaching for a prescription. One London general practitioner put it like this: 'patients do present to doctors with problems they're not trained to cope with. It's very difficult to respond in any other way than prescribing pills when you are presented with social and psychological problems day in day out, because the facilities are not available. I mean, if I wanted a patient to come off a tranquilliser now I would find it very difficult to provide them with alternative support.' In addition, many patients are as conditioned as doctors into *expecting* a prescription, and will leave the surgery with a sense of having being shortchanged without one. Doctors in Britain's socialised medical system ought to feel less pressure from this than they would if their livelihood depended on being popular with patients, as in America. But an unpopular doctor is also a bad doctor, since effective healing depends on a *two-way* sympathy between doctor and patient.

There are also many occasions when doctors may feel that a benzodiazapine tranquilliser is exactly fitted for the job in hand. Our North London doctor told us: 'I still prescribe benzodiazapines, I think they're excellent, superb, and they have just the desired effect ... I mean I prescribed some the day before yesterday to a lady who was travelling to Canada for the first time and terrified of travelling by air, but wanted to see her grandchildren.'

But it is noticeable even in this example, where the doctor is arguing for the *rational but restricted* use of the drug – agreeing for instance that he now realises 'they have a very, very limited role to play' – that he seems to be responding to a request for a particular drug: 'I would have thought it was terribly unfair of me to say "no, you can't have your lorazepam or diazepam".'

Tranquillisers and Women

It is no surprise that the subject of the Stones' song is 'Mother' and not 'Father', for women are given tranquillisers by their doctors twice as often as men. This *ought* to be surprising, since the problems for which the drug is given are not specific to women – social isolation, anxiety, the fear of growing old, insomnia can hit either sex. So why is it mainly women who are given tranquillisers?

A simple reason is that women go to the doctor more than men, and take more medicines of all kinds. But doctors also see the prescription of tranquillisers as particularly suitable for women's problems, a view that is reinforced in the way the drugs are marketed by the drug companies. A study of advertisements for 'mental health' drugs, for instance, has found that women appeared *fifteen times* more frequently in these than did men.

The author of the study, Gerry Stimson, commented that 'women's role-problems are defined in medical terms' and gives as an example a drugs advertisement which showed a harrassed housewife holding a tea-towel and standing next to a pile of dirty dishes. By trick photography the dishes are magnified to twice her size, while the text claims that the drug puts these problems 'into perspective'. In other words, women will stop *worrying* about the dishes and just get on with doing them! The attraction of this formula for the doctor (who is still usually a man) is that it is quicker and simpler to write a prescription than to discuss with the patient the possibility of buying a dishwasher, or getting the husband to do the dishes.

This raises an interesting question about the possible use of tranquillisers as a form of social control. *Soma* in *Brave New World* is quite deliberately given to the population for this purpose. Huxley says: 'The daily *soma* ration was an insurance against personal maladjustment, social unrest and the spread of subversive ideas.' The benzodiazapine tranquilliser has the same potential. Given systematically in cases of maladjustment and unrest amongst women, it is perfectly feasible to use it as a way of 'keeping them in their place'. A belief that this is actually happening on any scale, however, is for the conspiracy theorists. What can be said is that widespread tranquilliser use amongst women may very well have the effect of enabling them to live with unhappy situations, and so prevent them from reexamining and trying to change their lives.

As we shall discuss later, the doctor could offer far more constructive help by counselling the patient and referring her to another agency, which might help her to tackle her actual life problem directly. But most doctors still have neither the training nor the time to do this, and they may even be unaware of the scope which exists for referral to other supportive agencies. Instead they prescribe a drug which they hope will mask the difficulty, though all too often it merely creates a whole new set of problems, whilst leaving the original trouble unresolved.

Street Tranquillisers

Yet another factor in this equation is the growing frequency of *deliberate* benzodiazapine abuse – its use as a recreational drug. This is a very under-researched area, but it is clear that since the mid-1970s, tranquillisers have joined cannabis, heroin, amphetamines, Mandrax, LSD and glue as 'street drugs'.

Researching the illegal drugs trade, we have seen just how this works. Into a pub in London's Earl's Court comes a young man straight from a local doctor's surgery. This doctor is very accommodating, very easily convinced that such a patient has insomnia, 'exam nerves', depression brought on by unemployment or breaking up with a girlfriend. The result is a prescription for a month's supply of benzodiazapine. Chuckling at the doctor's gullibility, the man proceeds to sell the entire supply (at a pound a pill) in less than half an hour. The black market in these 'downers' depends mostly on prescription drugs acquired by deception. Some will be sold to hardened junkies, who inject them intravenously. They may be used for their intrinsic effect, or else to bring the user down from the high of another drug – cocaine, amphetamines or LSD.

Many 'ordinary' users of benzodiazapine tranquillisers may be surprised to hear that they share a habit with addicts and criminals. But because this is a psychoactive drug and causes dependence, the spillover from misuse into abuse and the black market is more or less inevitable.

Getting off Tranquillisers

The easy prescribing habits of the past survive in the continuing attitude of many doctors. Although tranquilliser prescriptions have fallen by 25 per cent in Britain since warnings about dependence were printed on the labels, it is still possible to find doctors who believe some patients, because of their condition, 'ought' to be on tranquillisers for life. There may be even more doctors, however, who would regard it as too difficult, or 'more trouble than it's worth' to take the patient off the drug. These views really cannot be justified any more, and in the light of what is now known would amount to gross irresponsibility.

Taking Tranquillisers

Apart from the severe withdrawal symptoms, there are other debilitating effects of continuing to use the drugs. Tina, we remember, was always in a state of heightened activity and nervousness. Long-term use may cause permanent damage to the nervous system. For instance, chronic benzodiazapine takers have lower scores in IQ tests than similar people who do not take them. Also, some benzodiazapine users have abnormal brain-scans, similar to, but not as marked as, changes found in the brain-scans of alcoholic patients. It is possible, of course, that the 'primary problems' of these individuals are the cause of these measurable abnormalities, but the suspicion remains that long-term use of benzodiazapines may cause brain damage.

It is therefore essential that patients who have been taking these drugs for more than four months should come off them. Withdrawal is often managed gradually, over a four- to twelve-week period – the most effective period of withdrawal has not yet been established. Patients on short-acting compounds might usefully switch to long-acting ones, so that the habit of pill-*taking* can be broken up as a first step to withdrawal. But this needs close supervision in case the user accidentally goes back to the old frequency, when an overdose could result.

Self-help Groups

Although most people are able to stop taking tranquillisers on their own and without too much difficulty, the longer they have been on them, the more likely it is that problems with withdrawal will occur. We have looked in some detail at the very painful withdrawal symptoms which can be caused, and the support and advice of people with first-hand experience of this can prove invaluable. This is the basis of the self-help approach.

Joan Jerome, herself a long-term user of tranquillisers, started the Tranx organisation in 1982, after she had gone through the difficult process alone, and before benzodiazapine dependence had received wide medical recognition. 'When I came off tranquillisers there was simply no help available', she told us, 'and I realised I couldn't be the only person who was swallowing Valium. So I decided that once I was better I would try and find these others and help them.'

Tranx now receives about 1,200 enquiries every month, and there are 500 groups around the country. She feels that much more help is needed and that Tranx's own effectiveness is limited by lack of resources. Nevertheless, the groups are effective. In Joan Jerome's local group in Middlesex, 90 per cent of the members do finally break the habit, although this can be a very long process. 'It partly depends on how many drugs you are taking. We don't believe in speeding the process up – it's up to each person to go their own pace. It's our philosophy that the slower the better, because it gives people time to adjust psychologically.'

Moira Hamblin, a Birmingham clinical psychologist running withdrawal groups inside the health service, also stresses the need to *relearn* life without tranquillisers. 'People need to get to know themselves, to understand why they started taking tranquillisers in the first place and to find other, positive ways of handling stress.' In our vocabulary, Moira is helping people deal with their primary problems as well as the secondary ones caused by the drug. This is crucial in all drug withdrawal treatment, as we shall see in the next chapter.

Moira also works with doctors to make them aware of other ways of helping people deal with anxiety, instead of doling out prescriptions for pills. Doctors need to be told or reminded of services to which they could refer patients. Tina, for instance, believes that, when she first went to the doctor all those years ago, what she really needed was help with her marriage problems: 'Ironically, there was a marriage guidance centre just up the road, and that's what I needed, someone to talk to, simple as that. Really my problems were social, not medical.' Yet, instead of referring her there for counselling, the doctor started her on a twenty-year path of drug dependence.

Schemes like the one in Birmingham are all too rare, and while increasing amounts of government money are spent on combatting heroin addiction, very little goes towards the tranquilliser problem, though this affects many more people. At the heart of the issue is a belief in the power of doctors and of medicines, which Ron Lacey of MIND thinks must now be broken down: 'We need to invest a lot of money in health education to tackle the pill culture, which patients as well as doctors subscribe to – this belief that there is a "pill for every ill". We need to stop being consumers in our own lives and start being participants.'

Ron Lacey also points out that, unlike that of alcohol or hard drugs, the tranquilliser compulsion is a private problem, often affecting women who are leading isolated and stressful lives at home, perhaps caring for young children or elderly relatives. A true *community* health service would reach out to these people at an early stage, and offer help with all the *hidden* problems that people take under the guise of other symptoms to their doctors. These commonly include difficulties with marriage, housing, child care, employment and *un*employment.

Such a service would demand much greater liaison between social workers and health services, and unfortunately government departments are notoriously bad at orchestrating such cooperation. But, idealistic as it may sound, we believe this sort of initiative would be effective, not just against tranquilliser misuse, but in combatting many of the compulsive problems dealt with throughout this book.

Chapter 4

Taking Heroin

It isn't the Horse, for all the melodramatic
talk about withdrawal symptoms. It is
the pale rider. *Alexander Trocchi*

The compulsions we have looked at so far are extensions of
conventional behaviour. Compulsive eaters, dieters and drinkers
simply push behaviour which is part of everybody's experience to
an extreme, while to the tranquilliser user, what could be more
natural than obeying doctor's orders? The use of illegal drugs,
however, is quite another matter.

Lena's Story

Lena's early life was full of questioning. 'When I was an adolescent
I always wanted to change the world. That was my thing, you
know. The government was wrong, the people in power were all
wrong. I felt I had this message to give the world.'

She was the seventh of eight children from a working-class
Greek Cypriot background. Her family aimed high: all her brothers
and sisters have become successful in their chosen careers.
Lena, however, was always the 'black sheep'.

She is a chronic asthmatic, and had a lot of therapeutic drugs
as a child, when she went in and out of hospital. Her first
experiments with illegal drugs came at the age of thirteen, and she
took LSD. When her mother found out Lena was for a while
'institutionalised' at an assessment centre. Undeterred, Lena's
self-image as the rebel of the family was now firmly established.

Her social circle all took drugs, and her best friend was thrown
out of school for dealing. Lena first experienced an opium-derived
drug when one of her friends gave her methadone. This changed
her life. She drank a large dose and 'from the very first time I knew
I was addicted, which was a very frightening experience'. She
graduated to heroin, which made her feel warm and secure, as

if nothing mattered. All the questions which had haunted her melted away. 'I felt adequate, that's the best way to describe it, and most of the time I'd felt inadequate ... When I used heroin I suddenly felt I could cope. And that whole mentality was how I knew I was going to be an addict.'

Lena speaks of her time as a heroin user as an obsessional love-affair with the needle. This is a common feeling amongst junkies, but at first, most users shy away from injecting themselves. Lena did not – she felt comfortable with it from the start, and believes this may have been because she had associated the hypodermic with being cared for during the times in childhood when she had stayed in hospital. Even in making her first attempt to come off heroin she used the needle to help her, deliberately injecting herself with the syringe of a friend whom she knew had hepatitis. In this way she successfully became infected, was admitted to hospital and 'dried out'.

She lived without the drug for two years. But then, as she was about to end an important relationship with a man, she took it again to 'give myself courage'. Soon she was back using heroin in her old, compulsive way. A further course of treatment six months later was quickly followed by another relapse. Two of her closest friends (also addicts) died, and Lena was herself now beginning to spiral down into the lower depths of drug-dealing, prostitution and increasing isolation.

Just in time, she pulled herself back; we shall hear how she was able to do so later. Although she now lives without heroin, she feels the need for continual support, always fearing the thought of slipping back. When we met her, she knew exactly how long she had been 'dry' – she had counted each passing day – 741 of them.

Heroin is no longer in her body, but it is still ever-present in her mind.

There are literally thousands of young (and not-so-young) people with stories like Lena's. In this chapter we shall concentrate on the problems of heroin, though the drug scene is an interrelated whole and users of one drug will nearly always consider taking any of the more or less dangerous street-drugs that are offered to them – cocaine and amphetamine (or 'speed') in particular. This polydrugging happens where users are habitual multiple-drug takers, and also where supplies of the chosen drug are low and substitutes are needed.

Compulsion

How Many Users Are There?

It is very difficult to know the extent of heroin use in Britain today, but it is generally recognised as an increasing problem. At the end of the 1950s there were no more than fifty registered addicts. The first wave of drug-taking amongst young people came in the 1960s, when heroin was an exotic and expensive drug. Nevertheless the number of addicts on the Home Office register climbed to 2,000. A second surge of interest in drugs coincided with the economic recession of the late 1970s, after which the number of notified addicts began to soar to a 1985 level of 14,688. This figure is now rising by 2,000 or 3,000 a year, but that increase does not reflect the true number of *new* notifications: addicts have a high death-rate and many of the names registered are not carried over from one year to the next. Half of all new notifications - perhaps 2,000 a year – are of people aged under twenty-five.

The register of notified addicts is compiled from information supplied by the police and the National Health Service. But it reflects only a small part of the heroin-using picture. It is estimated that for every notified addict, there are at least three compulsive heroin users whose names are not known to the authorities, and at least another four who are occasional users. Some of these at least will be on the way to a full-blown habit. So it is probable that at least 120,000 people in Britain today take heroin.

How Do Users Get Heroin?

During the early stages of the Ayatollah Khomeini's revolution in 1978 thousands of fleeing Iranians chose to bring their wealth out of Iran in the form of heroin, which was an ideal currency, having a higher weight-for-weight value than ten pound notes. Many of these refugees settled in or passed through Britain, and the drug has been cheap and plentiful here ever since. The bonanza of Iranian heroin came to an end, but it opened up a huge market for the drug, which has continued to be readily supplied, especially from producers in remote regions of Pakistan. Many of these use the proceeds to finance the anti-Russian guerrilla war in Afghanistan. So the user's 'score', in a pub or club somewhere in England, is the last link of a chain which reaches back to many of the political and military struggles of the Third World. Indeed it is partly the existence of these struggles that helps to ensure a plentiful and affordable supply.

62

Using Heroin

Most heroin is imported by criminals either in sophisticated organisations, smaller groups or as freelance individuals. They buy it cheaply in one of its countries of origin – most of these are in South-East Asia – smuggle it through British customs either using couriers or by concealing it in some more innocent shipment, and sell it (relatively) expensively. The profits are huge – around 4,000 per cent – and just as there are plenty of out-of-the-way places where the opium poppy will grow, so there is no shortage of groups, as diverse as the IRA, the Mafia and possibly even the secret services of unfriendly governments, who are prepared to act as importers.

Below these wholesalers there is a distribution network of middlemen and 'street dealers' – the distinction between the two is somewhat vague, although it is the latter who are known in the newspapers as 'pushers'. It is these dealers who strike the final street price which the addict must pay. Sales – or *scores* - are made by personal contact, or by frequenting places where dealing is known to go on. Pubs, cafes or clubs usually act as these unofficial drugs exchanges.

Heroin *smuggling* is not the only source. Notified addicts can be prescribed the drug, and some of these prescriptions also enter the black market. Then there are raids on pharmacies and doctors' surgeries, which yield further supplies.

What is Heroin?

In the world of its users, heroin has had many names – H, horse, junk, dope, gear, smack, scag. Officially it is *diamorphine hydrochloride*, a synthetic derivative from morphine, which itself is refined from opium. Heroin was first developed as a non-addictive substitute for morphine. Ironically, this new wonder-drug turned out to be far *more* addictive. As a painkiller, it is also far more effective than morphine.

Heroin is a soluble white or brown powder which tastes remarkably bitter and can be injected, smoked, swallowed or sniffed. It acts by affecting the brain cells directly. So, as a painkiller, it does not work by *blocking* painful impulses from reaching the brain, but simply by changing the state of mind in such a way that unpleasant impulses no longer feel unpleasant. In people who are not in any direct pain, this state of mind – induced by all morphine-based drugs – is in itself extremely pleasurable, and it is this very pure pleasure, initially at least, for which the user is looking.

The quality of this pleasure is hard, if not impossible, to define.

Compulsion

All perceptive descriptions of the heroin experience stress that it is a particularly *inward-turning* sensation. The Scottish addict and writer Alexander Trocchi described it as follows: 'the perceiving turns inward, the eyelids droop, the blood is aware of itself, a slow phosphorescence in all the fabric of flesh and nerve and bone ... the organism has a sense of being intact and unbrittle, and, above all, *inviolable*. For the attitude born of this sense of inviolability some Americans have used the word *cool*.' Rather less poetically, this 'self-absorbed' aspect of the heroin experience is known universally amongst addicts as 'nodding'.

Why Do People Start?

We saw with alcohol that consumption increases according to alcohol's availability, price and acceptability. The same rule applies to heroin. We have already seen how easy it is to get, so how cheap is it?

On the street, heroin now costs £80 to £100 per gram and the effective dose, for someone who has not built up tolerance, is five to ten milligrams. So, for the new user, a single fix should cost between five and ten pounds. The combination of availability and a low price is enough to make heroin use possible. But you must still *want* to take it.

Mary's Story

Mary was sixteen when she came to London. She knew very little about drugs of any kind, but she started going out with a boy who was a heroin user, although at first she did not know this. Mary became a heroin addict herself because 'my boyfriend knew people that were using. Then I started working in the West End and basically I had so much money that I didn't really know what to do with it. I'd seen people using it, and trying it wasn't really in my mind, but it just came around and I did try it.' When Mary joined her boyfriend's group of friends she entered a circle of hardened users, for whom heroin was a completely normal accessory to life. Being acceptable to these people meant not just taking the drug, but taking it in the preferred manner. 'First of all I started taking it at weekends, and then gradually it became an everyday thing. But I didn't start snorting it. I went straight to injecting, which made it a lot worse.' Within a few months Mary had become a heroin addict, and remained one for five years until her pregnancy prompted her to seek treatment.

Using Heroin

William Burroughs, the American cult author of several novels about heroin, has a dictum that 'you become a heroin addict because you do not have strong motivations in any other direction. Junk wins by default.' Although there are many factors in the long-term compulsion of heroin addiction, Burroughs's words certainly hold true in the way many people begin to take it. This can happen, as it did for Mary, in a process of imperceptible drift, a gradual entrancement with the drug, without any obvious motivation or deliberation.

Much popular indignation is directed at 'pushers' as the cause of heroin taking. The theory is that the dealer *gives* heroin to susceptible people just long enough to get them hooked, and then begins charging them for it. This is the more plausible because 'junk', as Burroughs says, 'is the ultimate merchandise. No sales talk necessary. The client will crawl through a sewer and beg to buy.' But the theory of pushing as the usual cause of drug addiction does not stand up. Burroughs's description of sewer-crawling clients applies only to well-established addictions, not recently-acquired habits. Besides, dealers are not necessarily the sharks they are portrayed. They often deal not for profit but merely to finance their own habits. And as Tom Field, an ex-addict, put it in his book *Escaping the Dragon*, 'many dealers ... turn away new clients, because more clients mean more risk. Equally, as a general rule, people are not introduced to heroin by a dealer but by their best friends. "Pushers" probably exist, but I have never come across one or met anyone who has.'

We have seen how both Lena and Mary were given heroin by boyfriends. The motives of these friends may be mixed – they might just want to share something which they believe is good, or they might conceivably enjoy 'corrupting' people. But it is unlikely that they do so for profit.

Heroin belongs to a subculture: people take it for the same reasons they want to join the subculture. In some ways the subculture seems glamorous. It is certainly associated with the entertainment industries, especially pop and rock music. It is also a very clear and drastic alternative to normal, bourgeois, establishment life. As such it can prove irresistible to young people who want to rebel against conformity, but have no 'strong motivations in any other direction'. The insider Tom Field confirms this: 'the majority of addicts admit to lacking any strong ambition before they tried heroin.'

Compulsion

The Compulsion to Continue

People easily form a close, compulsive relationship with heroin, as if with a person. Being introduced to people does not automatically mean that you will continue to see them, but the more attractive those people are, and the more they seem to like you, the more likely you are to seek them out. Even more so if you have problems that you know they will listen to. The same applies to heroin.

Heroin is very attractive, and it seems to like *you* very much. Heroin's gift is security and insulation from anything and everything – the 'inviolability' about which Alexander Trocchi wrote.

Of course it has its unattractive features. It affects your health in ways we will discuss later. Initially it may involve vomiting and the unpleasantness of using a hypodermic syringe. It is often adulterated with other substances. But none of these disadvantages seem to matter – in fact, as with people you love, the very drawbacks of the drug often become mixed up with its charm. We remember Lena's 'love affair' with the needle.

These are elements of the psychological compulsion, which grows as heroin-use grows. The extraordinary attractiveness of heroin ensures that – like *soma* - it inevitably becomes the object of compulsive behaviour for some people, even if there were nothing more to it. Unfortunately there is more to it.

Addiction and Dependence

The term 'addiction' has rather fallen from favour in the modern medical dictionary to be replaced by the more passive idea of 'dependence'. But in our everyday language we still use the word 'addiction' to describe compulsive behaviours such as the need to take a drug or bet on the horses. The name 'addict' can even be applied to innocuous activities such as going to the cinema or train-spotting. However the single action now most strongly associated with the word 'addict' is that of injecting heroin intravenously.

Using this everyday term, then, the compulsion to continue with heroin (as described above) is a 'psychological addiction'. Psychological addiction is the inability to shake off a habit, because the mind has become conditioned into expecting (and so desiring) to continue that habit. Most habits, as we saw in the introduction, are easily thrown off under the right circumstances. Addictions, however, are habits that have in some way acquired a peculiar grip on the psychological make-up of an individual, becoming integrated into the self-image in such a way that people find it literally impossible to imagine themselves without it. This kind of addiction is, in fact, indistinguishable from compulsion as we have been using the term.

There is also the matter of *physical* addiction. This also derives from the process of learning, but in this case it is a biological kind of learning. Biologists have given it another word – 'tolerance'.

Tolerance (as we saw in the case of alcohol) is the process whereby the cells of the body, by adapting themselves, learn to accommodate certain chemicals which are regularly introduced into the body – either alien substances or natural ones in unnaturally high quantities. If introduced to these substances over time, the cells of the body gradually integrate them into their own make-up. A certain amount of the substance present in the body becomes normal, so that if the amount is reduced withdrawal symptoms are felt. To abolish withdrawal symptoms, the substance must be reintroduced at once.

There is another physical consequence of using such a drug continuously over a period of time. As tolerance builds up, the noticeable effects of the drug gradually wear off, and it becomes part of the ordinary biological background. If users of a drug to which tolerance has been acquired wish to maintain the physical effects, they are soon faced with diminishing returns, since their bodies now treat the substance as a normal constituent. In this case the addict's only answer is to step up the dose.

These two elements – withdrawal symptoms and increased dosage – are regarded as the main signs of physical dependence. Both can be seen in their most extreme form in regular users of opium-derived drugs, because these are the most addictive substances known. Heroin is the most addictive of all.

Why Are Opiates So Addictive?

We have argued that there are no 'born' alcoholics, since alcohol is an alien substance whose use and misuse has to be learned. However, the situation with heroin and other opiates is rather more complicated and puzzling.

One important point about heroin has already been considered – that it *is* extremely pleasurable, and that the pleasure is a strangely personal one, with its 'nodding' introspection. It is noticeable how many addicts speak of the instant recognition they experienced with the drug, as if they had found a missing part of themselves. Lena, for instance, had no doubts – 'from the very first time I knew I was an addict'. It is as if she was destined to be a junkie.

Is there any more truth in this than in the idea of an inborn disease called 'alcoholism'? The most convincing evidence about this has come from recent scientific work on the chemistry of the brain. In the last fifteen years substances known as *endorphins* have been discovered. These are products of the brain and the nervous system, and they duplicate many, if not all, of the effects of opiates. These biological opiates seem to be involved in natural pain-control, and also in pleasure. Their production is doubled and redoubled during sex, for example. The similarity between opiates and endorphins seems to be confirmed by the action of a drug called *naloxone* which has been known for a long time as the antidote to opium: it has now been found to reduce natural pain control also. The fact that naloxone is the antidote to opiates *and* to endorphins is very strong evidence of structural similarities between the two substances.

There is another fact about the endorphins which may be relevant here. Their concentrations in the body are highly variable from one individual to another, as if some people have a greater capacity to produce them than others. So there may be a difference in susceptibility to heroin – an *addiction gap* – between those who produce a lot of natural opiates and those who make less.

If the similarity between opiates and the endorphins is real, it is nevertheless accidental, a coincidence of chemical shape. But it does mean that heroin, when it enters the body, is immediately recognised biologically, and this must give it an in-built advantage over other psycho-active drugs. There is a difference between someone who arrives at a house as a total stranger, and another who is carrying papers to show he is a long-lost son of the family. The similarity of heroin and endorphin means that we are all 'tuned' to the effects of heroin in a way we cannot be to alcohol – we seem to recognise it, and therefore the process of learning (in a biological sense) how to acommodate it is less difficult.

This does not remove the central role which ordinary learning plays in acquiring the heroin habit. Before you can become a compulsive user, you must first try it. Before you try it you must be *willing* to try it. And even before that, you must be able to learn how you are going to try it.

The Heroin User's Life

Heroin is a drastic drug in every sense. If taking it can be dramatically pleasant, its consequences are dramatically and un-compromisingly unpleasant, and this is one of the last and cruellest links in the chain of dependence. The changes which heroin-use brings about in a user's life can be so disastrous that the only recourse for some people is to keep on with ever-increasing doses of the drug itself. What causes the problem also solves the problem, making a circle which can seem impossible to break. One addict put it succinctly to Tom Field that 'smack starts as a carrot and ends as a stick.' Yet even as it beats, it dangles the carrot again.

Most of the problems arise from two overriding facts about the addict's world. First, it is completely dominated by the need to ensure a daily supply of the drug; nothing is allowed to interfere with this objective. The second fact is its criminality. As purchaser and possessor of heroin the user is a criminal amongst criminals, a member of an underworld where 'normal' standards do not necessarily apply. These facts affect addicts' health and life-expectancy, their friendships and their relations with their family.

Health

Heroin is a depressant many times stronger than alcohol. In overdose it causes a deepening coma until, eventually, the brain-centre which controls the breathing reflex shuts down. The user then dies of asphyxiation.

In regular use, heroin's automatic physical effects are con-sequences of its depressant action: chronic constipation, difficulty in passing urine and in sexual ejaculation, hormonal disturbance and contraction of the pupils of the eye. Breathing becomes shallow and the heart slows. The drug itself, unlike alcohol, does not seem to damage the body's tissue directly, perhaps because (as discussed above) it so resembles the natural endorphins. But it can do indirect damage. For example by suppressing the cough-reflex, heroin can lead to lung infections. Also, because the body mistakes heroin for endorphin, it cuts back its own endorphin production to such an extent that, eventually, the body is producing no natural endorphin at all. Not enough is known about the action of endorphins to be sure what harm, if any, this may do. It may explain why addicts experience so much itching.

The way of life of the addict also takes its toll on health. Looking after yourself in a conventional sense takes second place to looking after yourself in a heroin sense. Users usually have an inadequate diet, they lose weight, and their skin becomes pallid.

Compulsion

Apart from this, addicts who inject have particular health problems. The state of their veins, after a long period of use, becomes extremely precarious, sometimes collapsing completely. This naturally causes blood-circulation disorders. Addicts may also accidentally inject air or some other foreign body into the vein, resulting in a 'dirty fix' which, according to Tom Field, results in 'violent bouts of shivering, so violent that it is impossible, for example, to drive. After a few hours in bed, however, the effects pass.' There is also an ever-present possibility of infection from water used to dissolve the heroin, and from dirty needles. Addicts rarely sterilise anything: if they clean their needle at all it is in water. If the user is injecting into a vein, the whole 'works' – syringe and needle – inevitably become contaminated with blood, because blood is drawn in to check that a vein has been hit. In health terms, sharing their works is the most dangerous thing addicts can do.

The most common serious illness affecting addicts is *serum hepatitis*. We saw how Lena deliberately gave herself hepatitis from a friend's works in order to help her get off heroin. Hepatitis is a virus which infects the liver: one case in ten presents a serious threat to life. In malnourished addicts, whose immune systems are working well below par, the illness is much worse than usual.

But the new menace of Acquired Immune Deficiency Syndrome (AIDS) is far more serious. Nobody knows how many people infected with the AIDS virus will eventually die from the disease – estimates have varied from 15 to 100 per cent. What is certain is that heroin addicts are among the two highest-risk groups. In New York there are a quarter of a million heroin addicts, and it is believed that 150,000 are already infected with the virus. In Italy three-quarters of addicts have the virus; in France, 70 per cent; in Sweden, 50 per cent; in Spain, 48 per cent. In Britain, where syringes are probably easier to obtain than elsewhere, at least 10 per cent of heroin addicts (as opposed to occasional users) are AIDS carriers – more than 8,000 people.

If addicts can avoid all these hazards, and as long as a steady supply of heroin is available, they will suffer no great health problems. But when the heroin runs out, their whole body goes into a state of open revolt.

First it starts working on overdrive. Because heroin suppresses vital functions, the addict's body automatically balances this suppression by raising its work-rate. If heroin-input then ceases, the body has nothing to fight against and the automatic body functions are suddenly working to excess: the eyes and nose run, there is yawning and copious sweating, diarrhoea, fever, shivering and gooseflesh. The mood is also depressed and pains appear all over the body, probably to do with the shortage of endorphins. In summary, the addict with withdrawal symptoms has a flu-like illness that can last one or two weeks, unless another dose of heroin, or another opiate such as methadone, is taken. Then the symptoms disappear at once.

Because these symptoms resemble a bad dose of flu, some users fail to recognise them. After Mary had been using for six months, she went to her doctor with what she thought was flu. The doctor recognised them as withdrawal symptoms from heroin, and told her he could not offer her treatment. She must choose, he said, between continuing to feel ill and continuing with heroin. She went back to the needle.

Social Life

Every addict agrees that heroin-use changes your personality. Essentially this is because it withdraws you from interest in anything other than the drug. As William Burroughs puts it, the narcotics addict becomes a vegetable: 'The addict is immune from boredom. He can look at his shoe for hours or simply stay in bed. He needs no sexual outlet, no social contacts, no work, no diversion, no exercise, nothing but morphine.'

However, because of his need for the drug, the addict *does* have a social life, though it is strictly for the instrumental purpose of keeping in touch with supplies of the drug. The world of narcotics addiction is quite unlike that of other drug users, it seems, because it is utterly without illusions. Again, Burroughs puts this better than anyone. In *The Naked Lunch* he says: 'All the hallucinogenic drugs are considered sacred by those who use them ... but no one ever suggested that junk is sacred. There are no opium cults. Opium is profane and quantitative, like money.' Although the relationship to heroin is like a cloying friendship, the addict's ambivalence about the drug is clearly reflected in the ugliness of many slang terms for it: it is 'shit', 'scag' and 'junk'.

Personal friendships in the addict's world are also ambivalent. They can be deeply dependent, but only if this props up the dependence on the drug. The need to obtain the drug overrides all other allegiances. As Alexander Trocchi tells us, 'there is a confederacy amongst users, loose, hysterical, traitorous, unstable, a tolerance that comes from the knowledge that it is very possible to arrive at the point where it is necessary to lie, cheat and steal, even from a friend who gave one one's last fix.' The chaotic and ultimately fatal triangular relationship between punk rock star Sid Vicious, his girlfriend Nancy Spungeon and heroin had all these hallmarks.

Morality for the junkie goes out of the window. In this, he resembles certain other compulsives, such as those suffering from eating disorders. Except when made careless by the onset of withdrawal, the narcotics user is adept at concealing his condition, or, at least, at telling convincing lies about it. There is an element of the survival of the fittest in this. The user who does not learn to lie and cajole in order to get money for heroin is less 'successful' in the shark-pool. And while the addict can be extremely self-pitying and self-abasing when in need of a fix (pride having joined morality in the rubbish bin), his heart is probably hardened against an equivalent plight in others.

Another way in which heroin changes the personality of users is by making them criminals. Not only are they *prima facie* law-breakers, they are often forced into crimes like stealing, fraud and prostitution just to get money to buy the drug. Holding down a job is extremely difficult because of the immensely time-consuming business of buying heroin. The addict's life is very often a nocturnal one, which does not fit with a daytime job. When Mary started shoplifting to help pay for heroin, she was arrested and put on remand for three weeks, the first four days of which were spent withdrawing in the prison hospital wing. When she came out there was little or no follow-up or support – and a six-week wait for an appointment at a drug-treatment centre. In the meantime she went back to heroin.

Being known to the police as an addict leads to endless problems. Mary told us that she was on 'first name terms' with the police: 'It just became, like, every day. They were always stopping us, looking for stuff, and they knew who I was straight away. It didn't matter how many times I tried to change, they just knew ... In a week, I'd be down there three or four times for different offences.'

Family

As the addict's life becomes focused on heroin to the exclusion of everything else, the compulsion grows into an impassable barrier between the addict and the 'straight' world. Non-users show little understanding or tolerance of heroin addiction and this lack of sympathy is not alleviated by the frequently antisocial behaviour of users. For one group of 'straights', the addict's own family, this becomes especially distressing.

Gayle's Story

Gayle took heroin for fifteen years. She successfully hid it from her family for several of those years, mainly by staying away from them. 'I would only go to visit them when I was on my best form – I wouldn't go to see them sick, and I always put on as good a front as I possibly could.'

But there came a point when Gayle realised that her parents knew. Nothing was said, however; it was a conspiracy of silence. 'We both made the decision it seems, that neither of us was going to admit it. In fact once I'd spent the weekend with my sister, who's a nurse, and she'd found the works in my bag. She rang up my mother to tell her. My mother knew it but she said "No, it's not that" – she totally denied it.'

David Smith, a probation officer from Walton in Liverpool, is chairman of a local Family Support Group, a self-help organisation of about forty families and friends of drug-users. He told us that the disbelieving reaction of Gayle's parents is common, although behind it is a shattering trauma. 'When parents find out there is a drug abuser in the family, they're absolutely devastated. A great feeling of fear, guilt, shame, isolation and that feeling of not being able to do anything about it at all. So you just try to blank it out completely and pretend it's not there – until it's actually forced upon you.'

The stigma of having an addict in the family is not surprising. Addicts often admit to being outlaws or outcasts – that image is part of the spurious 'glamour' of addiction, though the glamour is an outsider's fantasy: addicts don't see glamour, just degredation. Junkies' lives are so much against the grain of straight society that they have become Untouchables, their presence an embarrassment on both sides. The result is a very unhappy situation. A child is alienated from the family just when their support is most needed.

Problems

Compulsions, we have argued, always have another problem, a *life* problem, behind them. The compulsive problem masks the original problem and overwhelms it; the need to satisfy the compulsion is so great that the original problem is left trailing behind in a person's list of priorities.

We have also said that many therapists now stress the need to deal with the primary problem before, or at least simultaneously with, the compulsion itself. But does the heroin compulsion fit this pattern?

Serious eating and dieting compulsions often derive from traumatic, loveless childhoods, and difficulties in making the transition to adulthood. Alcohol problems, too, come out of problems of adjustment and the need to *cope* with emotional knots in a person's life, while tranquillisers are given to people who seek help in coping with anxiety and depression. With heroin addicts, however, it often seems much more difficult to identify what has 'gone wrong' with their lives. It may simply be chance which leads a person to fall in with one group of friends rather than another – heroin users rather than, say, gamblers or glue-sniffers. But there ought to be more to it than accident. This compulsion has such a strong grip, is so drastic, that heroin users seem like freaks, abnormal even by contrast with other compulsives.

Tom Field says on this subject: 'One of the misconceptions about heroin is that no one who is "normal" could possibly take it, let alone become addicted to it. In other words, that heroin taking is only a symptom of delinquency. Certainly it is almost always symptomatic of some other "problem", but so often these "problems" are not the problems of delinquency but the problems of everyday life to which everyone is subject.'

Probably the remark quoted from William Burroughs earlier on comes closest to identifying what draws people into the heroin compulsion. It does not have to be a screaming mental agony, or a tortured existential choice, but merely the lack of 'strong motivation in another direction'. Boredom, emptiness, alienation have been recognised for most of this century as the price some people pay for materialism, industrialisation and urban living.

But this is a negative and nebulous complaint. Is the strength and destructiveness of the heroin compulsion not out of all proportion to it? Well, that is the point. Heroin is far more physically compelling than alcohol or cream cakes or tranquillisers. Taking it is like tinkering with an unexploded bomb so devastatingly sensitive that no more than the weakest, most negative life problem will set it ticking. Once it does start, of course, the bomb's own momentum and logic take over the user's life. All users start by thinking they can control heroin: the more they believe this the more likely it will end by controlling them. As Burroughs says, there is nothing mystical about it, and nothing (in spite of its name) heroic. It is hard and profane, 'like money'.

Coming Off

It is not impossible for an addict to come off heroin and the physical withdrawal symptoms are no worse than a dose of flu. But psychologically it *is* very difficult for it involves unlearning a whole way of life. There is much controversy over the best ways of doing this, but in the end they all centre round three things: first, removing the psychological *lift* which the drug gives; second, removing the physical dependence; and third, reentering straight society as a non-addict.

Assuming for instance that you are a heavy addict who uses a syringe. You can be distanced from the psychological pleasure of heroin by taking a 'maintenance dose' of methadone, another opiate which is taken orally. Methadone prevents withdrawal symptoms whilst removing the 'rush' of pleasure which even the most tolerant and habituated intravenous user experiences when he injects. Free methadone programmes exist in the United States, Holland and Britain, but there can be problems. A heroin user who takes methadone is merely converting himself to a methadone addict; without a very strong motivation (the kind of motivation lacking in most long-term addicts) there is a strong temptation to go back to heroin if it becomes available. It might also be remembered that Lena *began* her heroin career by drinking methadone.

However, once the addict has negotiated physical withdrawal (called 'cold turkey' because of the way it chills the skin and raises gooseflesh), the bodily craving, at least, is abolished. But it is not yet time for the ex-addict to return to society. The lack of heroin leaves a gigantic void in the user's life. As Gayle told us, her whole reality had been a 'drug reality'. Once that has gone, something else must be put in its place. This is even more urgent if the person's original state of mind, the *primary* problem which led to the heroin compulsion, was a feeling of emptiness, worthlessness and boredom. Any ex-addict who is rehabilitated, yet feels bored, alienated, unloved and useless will know exactly where to turn for a remedy: back to heroin.

So the addict wanting to break the dependence on heroin requires, above all, *support*.

Compulsion

The Crisis

Many, if not most, long-term heroin users sooner or later reach a point of crisis when they realise their habit is destroying them. Often this is triggered by outside events, especially trouble with the law. The first time Mary was prompted to seek help was when she 'needed a rest' because she 'had too many court cases coming up'. But we have already seen how unsympathetic, in her case, the family doctor was. In fact she has come to believe that 'GPs don't want to know. As soon as you tell them that you're a drug addict, the ones I know, they just don't care.'

This can be a real difficulty. Dr John Strang, Director of the Drug Dependency Unit at the Maudsley Hospital in London, told us that while there are certainly some GPs who will help with drug problems, 'the number who are willing to become involved is extremely small'. Many family doctors find it hard to sympathise with drug-users, and very often so do the staffs of hospital casualty departments. They feel their service is for people who cannot help being sick, and are tempted to dismiss heroin users as the authors of their own condition.

To cope with the dramatic recent increase in narcotics use, efforts must be made to change the doctor's perceptions of the drug addict. But this on its own will not be enough. In an attempt to make it easier for drug-users to seek medical help, Dr Strang has been involved in setting up community drug teams. These are staffed by non-medical people who work to ease communications between users and doctors, and may involve others, too, such as probation officers and social workers. Such teams provide the hope of a more all-round back-up to the medical treatment which the user needs. This is still at a very experimental stage: if it works, it will need many more resources to make it widely available.

There is also a role for specialist *drugs crisis centres*. London's City Roads is such a place – it has a mere twelve beds where users can stay for three weeks and 'detoxify'. City Roads takes in 250 people each year, and helps another 4,000 through telephone counselling. It has a staff of thirty and is open twenty-four hours a day.

City Roads is a valuable resource, and many more such centres are needed. But it can only offer a breathing space; there are no after-care facilities. Many mothers with babies have to be turned away because there is no accommodation for children. Half the people City Roads sees are living rough, and in the end, all too soon, these drug-users will have to return to their earlier way of life. As one of the staff at City Roads put it, 'if drug-users are asked to swap oblivion for awareness, and that awareness is only of the hopelessness of their situation, how can we blame them for choosing oblivion?'

For Lena the crisis which drove her to take treatment came from within her family. It was her mother whose sympathetic concern gave her the courage to seek help, and Lena completed six months as an out-patient at a drugs clinic, coming off the drug with the help of methadone. However, she knew that she needed even longer-term support than this – the kind of support provided at Phoenix House.

Making Phoenixes

The phoenix is a mythical bird who was said to be reborn out of its own ashes. Phoenix Houses are long-stay rehabilitation centres for addicts whose lives have been reduced to ashes. There are houses in London, Merseyside, Tyneside and Yorkshire.

The philosophy of Phoenix House is that of the 'therapeutic community', which was pioneered in the 1960s by R. D. Laing and others for treating schizophrenics. The essence of the Phoenix House approach is that the drug-user – who nearly always comes there out of desperation – makes a commitment to live for twelve months with others in the same situation. Half the staff are former addicts who have themselves been through the course.

It is a very 'tough' course, with an emphasis on routine and on a return to personal responsibility backed up by counselling and group-work. Lena admits she 'fell in love' with Phoenix House. It seemed to give her a framework within which she could start to rebuild her life. 'I actually got up in the morning, and I wasn't getting up just to have a fix. I was getting up and cleaning the room, I was taking responsibility for my life for the first time in God knows how long. All I knew before, when I was using, was how to destroy myself, and all of a sudden I was being taught how to be a productive human being. I have a lot of love for Phoenix House.'

The Phoenix House approach has been criticised for its un-compromising insistence on commitment, since the inability to make commitments is often at the heart of a heroin user's problem. But for those who can make that commitment, the process clearly enables drug-users at the very end of their tether to face both the drug problem itself, and the underlying life problems which have given rise to it. Not surprisingly, the emotional backgrounds which the courses uncover are often ones of break-up and deprivation. Many of the residents have arrived homeless. Many grew up in broken families or in care, or had unsettled childhoods, where the family perhaps moved house a good deal (as happens in the armed services), making it impossible for a child to form lasting relationships.

Having formed a twelve-month relationship with the community at Phoenix House, however, the residents have to move on again. This prompts another crisis which no amount of preparation can completely abolish. Peter Martin, the London director of Phoenix, told us what happens after the twelve months is up. 'We do keep tabs on most of the people that go through the programme, we run an after-care support group for approximately three-to-six months after people leave us. We encourage people to come back, and people do stay very much in touch. And we have social occasions too – people come back for barbecues in the summer, which also has a very positive effect on the community that is with us at the moment.'

For Lena the transition to everyday life was difficult, and she finds she still needs Phoenix House, or something rather like it. 'I still have quite a lot of contact with the community, to work there as well as to get support for myself. But I'm very enthusiastic about my life at the moment. I'm studying and I do quite a lot of community work. And I regularly go to a self-help group for ex-drug users.' The social life that Lena has found without drugs is nevertheless still rather a confined one. Now, instead of being constantly in the company of addicts, she spends much of her time with *ex*-addicts, which is not, perhaps, complete rehabilitation. Yet Lena's optimism is justified. She has climbed a mountain on her way to recovery and self-discovery and has, she says, learned from it 'a kind of acceptance and joy, and that it's okay not to be in control all the time.' Such an insight is a major step out of any compulsion.

Prevention

The prevention of narcotics compulsion is a massive international and national question.

The world's heroin trade is a virtually unregulated multi-billion dollar business. But it is important to remember that international drugs trafficking is not only to do with greed, it has much to do also with *need* – the economic deprivation of Third World countries. The opium poppy grows in some of the world's poorest soil, and profits for the grower are higher than they would be for any other comparable cash-crop. Therefore poor Third World countries will continue producing opium as long as they continue to be poor. The same applies to cocaine. So for affluent northern economies, where the worst social consequences of the narcotics trade are felt, effective control means making some hard choices. These will have to include eliminating some of the grosser inequalities of the world economy. But such questions are way beyond the scope of this book.

Nationally the problem of preventing drug abuse is also a difficult and controversial one. As an example of the divergence of opinion, the British government's recent advertising campaigns have been held up by many politicians as a significant contribution to the fight against hard drugs. On the other hand, many workers in the addiction field have criticised the campaign for inadvertently glamorising the drug and its subculture. One of the posters in a recent series has featured a photograph of a young male addict over the caption 'Heroin Screws You Up'. We have been told that some heroin users pin this poster up in their bedrooms as a kind of ikon.

Pam Shickler of the Teachers' Advisory Council on Alcohol and Drug Education (TACADE) believes that teachers and parents need to take a much more radical approach to teaching about drugs. TACADE produces materials for even quite young children which look at the role of drugs in our society and try to give accurate information about safety and health. 'We're a drug-using society', she says, 'and children need to know about chemicals in the home, the drugs people use – caffeine, solvents, nicotine, and alcohol as well as the hard drugs. We also teach the skills that go with this. How to take decisions, to communicate better with people, simply to live in the community. Teaching these life skills as part of health education can have an effect on reducing drug abuse.'

The TACADE approach is very much in line with this book's view of compulsions, as being part of a general attitude to life, and an attempt at problem-solving. We believe that the treatment and prevention of drug abuse must take into account the individual's whole life, aims and motivations, not solely the problems arising from the drug itself. We will explore this *holistic* approach in our final chapter.

Chapter 5

Working

See Saw, Margery Daw,
Johnny has got a new master;
He shall have but a penny a day
Because he can't work any faster.

The subjects of the next two chapters are rather different from the compulsions discussed so far. They do not concern *substances* that we consume compulsively – food, or different kinds of drugs – but *activities* or *feelings* which can exert such a hold over us that they dominate our lives just as powerfully as any drug.

Work can become such an activity, so compulsive that the term 'workaholic' has been coined to describe such people; there are signs that, in a society like ours, so much emphasis is put on achievement and success that the number of workaholics is growing. A recent example is young people employed on the London Stock Exchange who, since the arrival of computerised share dealing (the so-called 'Big Bang') are said to work more than twelve hours a day until they 'burn themselves out' after ten years of frantic and stressful activity.

Before we examine compulsive working, we need to look at the role of work in our lives. In Western society, the protestant work ethic has enormous prestige. We are brought up to believe that to be established in regular paid work is one of the highest moral achievements and this, particularly for men, justifies our existence and gives us status and a sense of our identity. Meanwhile idleness and lack of employment are seen as evil: 'the devil finding work for idle hands.'

This is one of the reasons why unemployment brings misery to most people. Of course, it does result in shortage of money and a sense of frustration, but it also carries a social stigma. People on the dole are considered to be scroungers, parasites who aren't pulling their weight in society. When people have worked for a large part of their adult lives, the sudden onset of retirement or redundancy can produce extreme side-effects similar to the withdrawal symptoms described in previous chapters. One man told Beatrix Campbell in her book *Wigan Pier Revisited*:

'I never go out, never see my friends … Sometimes I think my brain is dying. I get depressed – sometimes I shout and bawl. I'm not going mental, but I feel I might like to damage somebody … It's very difficult to get motivated. I've got a lot to do, like re-doing the kitchen, but I can't.'

In a series of articles for the *British Medical Journal* on the health of the unemployed Dr Richard Smith listed some of the psychological symptoms of unemployment as 'anxiety, depression, insomnia, irritability, lack of confidence, listlessness, inability to concentrate and general nervousness'. They really do resemble withdrawal symptoms.

Most adults have some kind of compulsion to work, or at least feel a strong *need* to do so, whether this is a paid job outside the home or the domestic work which many women do looking after children and men. Provided such work is available this need is entirely without problems. It is a perfectly acceptable way of seeking personal fulfilment, whose benefits (apart from the income) can be summarised in four points:

(1) Work structures our time.

(2) It enlarges our social relations beyond the family and neighbourhood.

(3) It gives the satisfaction of collective effort and achievements which are greater than anything we could do on our own.

(4) It gives us social status and a sense of who we are.

Each of these aims, however, can become distorted or exaggerated into a much more intense kind of compulsive behaviour and it is this compulsion – that of the 'workaholic' – with which we shall be concerned in the rest of this chapter.

Peter's Story

Peter is in his early forties. Happily married with children, a horse, a flock of sheep, a duck-pond and a beautiful nineteenth-century Cheshire farmhouse, he is the technical director of a chemical firm. 'Typical middle management', he calls himself, responsible to the managing director and a large sales force. Everything in the family's life seemed to be going extremely well until eighteen months ago, when without warning Peter had a heart attack.

> It was the first time I'd been in hospital since I was three. I was very grateful for all the care and attention I received whilst in hospital, but I was terribly scared. Why was this happening to me? It wasn't fair. I didn't smoke, or drink much, and there were plenty of people I knew who did, and weren't lying in hospital. I felt as though I'd let everybody down.

Peter's wife Pat believes that it was a phone call from the office the weekend before which triggered his attack. Peter was very wound up and tense after it, and later complained of feeling ill. During the following week he collapsed at the office. Peter agrees that worry about work tended to dominate much of his spare time, when he was unable to be *doing* it. 'I used to worry about the small things, the things I hadn't achieved that day at work, things that really weren't in my power to change. I'd wake up in the middle of the night and all my troubles would come to the fore.'

Peter had always been a compulsive worker. As a younger man he had been a salesman 'in the field' and had maintained an office at home. He would retire into this room for hours during what should have been his 'leisure time' and work – even, Pat recalls, on Boxing Day. He could not really enjoy holidays, he had little appreciation of incidental pleasures: things had to relate back to work, or they did not get a second glance.

In his work he would take anything and everything on board in a blind, unquestioning way, not willing to admit that some things were not in his domain. He could hardly bear to delegate. Frustration and tension would build up and often could not be discharged. Because of this he was in a more or less constant state of nervous anxiety. Exactly, as we shall see, the physical state which can lead to heart and other health problems and one of the possible penalties of being a workaholic.

Workahol

Peter admits he was a workaholic. Obviously enough, the very word was invented to underline the analogy with alcoholism. It implies that the activity of working, like drinking alcohol, can take hold of a person so strongly that it overwhelms his or her life, at the expense of all other satisfactions. But how strong is this analogy?

In our alcohol chapter we saw that drinking alcohol is a *learned* activity, and that even at social levels it has compulsive characteristics. In fact, 'normal' work is probably more compulsive than 'normal' drinking, since, as we have seen, its withdrawal often leads to serious mental health problems, which are in some ways similar to the withdrawal symptoms of drug addicts. So much for 'normal' work and drinking. In what ways does the workaholic resemble the problem drinker and other compulsives?

We have identified two aspects of compulsive behaviours which mark them as potentially destructive – the mask and the lash. Workaholics are perhaps most obviously employing a lash on themselves. Workaholic executives like Peter meet a 'punishing' schedule of travel, meetings, number-crunching and dictation. But they still lack satisfaction. Like an addict without a fix, they lie in bed mentally working, haunted by thoughts of loose-ends not tied up, committees that could have gone better, memos that might have been badly worded. Almost any primary problem might lie beneath this type of behaviour, any residual guilt which needs expiation.

Compulsive work also makes an ideal mask, for it is a complete persona, leaving little or no room for expression in other directions. Peter, well on the way to achieving a less compulsive way of working, has had to change for the sake of his health – to survive, in fact. Pat has noticed that he is now much more open to experience: 'Obviously making a change like this, you can't do everything at once, but there is a gradual awareness of things around him. For instance we were going away on holiday, and he was able to remark on the view. It may sound a small thing, but just to be able to be aware of things means an awful lot.' The old Peter had never been aware, at least in this sense of being 'open to experience'. He was like a blinkered racehorse, his 'mask' forcing his eyes forward towards a far-off (and ever-receding) finishing post. Such a mask has the double use of enabling you to forget the existence of the people around you, and of preventing *them* from seeing who *you* really are.

Similar evasions, as we have seen, are found in many problem drinkers, bulimics and drug-takers; work can be used (or abused) to similar ends.

Some psychologists believe that certain *types* of people are more likely to use work as their preferred form of coping behaviour, and more likely to slip into the 'abuse' of work.

Compulsion

Type A and Type B People

Two American heart specialists, Meyer Friedman and Ray Rosenman, were the first to notice the odd behaviour of heart patients in the consulting room. Most patients claim they cannot get enough of their doctor's time, but here the situation was reversed. Friedman and Rosenman found they were being hustled through their consultations by patients who looked repeatedly at their watches, seemed wound up and eager to get away and would eventually terminate the discussion by mentioning a pressing business engagement.

Friedman and Rosenman decided this kind of *hurrying* and *worrying* individual must be particularly prone to heart disease, because they were seeing so many of them. As cardiologists, they decided to enquire further into the phenomenon. Not to saddle the enquiry with any emotive terms, they gave it a deliberately neutral tag: they called it the 'Type A' personality. In the sketch below we have characterised the Type A as a man, but in fact women are just as likely to fit the type as men.

Meyer and Friedman found their waiting room seats were worn only at the front edge. This was because the Type A hates to wait; he is permanently 'on the edge of his seat'. He cannot sit back and relax, but is always poised on the brink of a renewed burst of activity. He becomes unbearably tense if delayed, and is very intolerant of others. This makes him appear highly competitive and aggressive. He is usually in the middle of two or more activities simultaneously.

This type of man is also difficult to converse with. He is always anticipating what you want to say, and finishing your sentences for you. He talks fast, walks fast, drives furiously, eats and runs, gulps his drinks, smokes in quick puffs.

Dr Terry Looker is a lecturer in the physiology of the heart and the circulation at Manchester Polytechnic. Because of its connection with heart disease, Dr Looker has become a leading authority on Type A behaviour. He told us that 'the Type A person has a series of beliefs and habits which mean that he perceives situations as threatening to him, and often this is inappropriate to the situation.' There can be an intensification of this condition which Dr Looker calls *speed-up*, where the sensation of threat mounts, and the Type A resorts to extreme measures. He will write memos during meetings or use two phones at the same time. Non-productive activities are even more ruthlessly dealt with. Some men have *two* electric shavers for simultaneous use. We have even heard of a man who always had an electric blender beside him at table. When his wife served a meal he would tip the food into the blender, press the *liquidise* button and drink the result, simply to save time.

The Type A classification is not exact. There are many shades and levels of Type A behaviour, and the point at which it turns into its opposite (or negative), which Friedman and Rosenman call Type B, is not clearly defined. Rather there is a continuous scale of behaviour between Types A and B, with no obvious boundaries in between. At the extreme of Type B there is the person with very little drive or ambition and a general appearance of torpid detachment. As behaviour approaches nearer to Type A there is the type who is simply relaxed, followed by the person who is alert and active, and then by the mildly stressed individual. Behaviour falls increasingly into the Type A classification as it goes through the stages of being chronically stressed, anxious and hurried and on into the phenomenon of 'speed up'.

What this implies, of course, is that the nearer you get to either extreme of behaviour the more problems you generate in your life. The recommendation ought then to be that people should remain in the middle range between relaxation and alertness. Not everyone agrees with this prescription, however; some believe that they function best as Type A workaholics.

Helen's Story

Knowing that many doctors are also workaholics we advertised in the *British Medical Journal*. Helen phoned us very quickly and said 'Yes, I'm a workaholic', but before we could pursue the conversation she said something had come up, and could she ring us back later! Fortunately, she did.

Helen is a hospital consultant in her mid-fifties. She is married with four grown children and is a self-confessed Type A personality. What she does *not* admit to is having problems from this. She told us 'I'm not competitive, in fact I can't stand competitions. If there is a competition then I retire. I either have to be best or very good, or I won't do it at all. I'm a typical Type A. I like stress, and I can't work unless it's under stress. I tend to do things at the last minute, but I like that.'

I like to do two things at the same time. When I was young I used to practise trying to *think* two things at once. Quite often when I was taking an exam, I'd try and learn something new at the same time, like playing the guitar – because I needed something to take my mind off what I was doing.

All through my life people have said things like 'You're not a proper woman, you're a career woman and you'll never get married', so I got married. Then they said 'You'll never have children', so I had four. Then they said 'Middle aged women with four kids have nothing to offer', so I went back to work and became a consultant in five years ... I always felt secretly that it was not OK to be a workaholic, until I read a book which told me that it *was*, so now I'm happy.

I now think there are two types of workaholics: physiological ones like me, who work hard and enjoy it and cope well, and pathological ones, who become very ill and find it paralyses them and makes life impossible. I think that provided I like it it's OK, and if *you* don't like what I'm doing, that's your problem, not mine!

So Helen, while certainly compulsive about work, does not feel this is a problem. There is a school of thought which supports her. It suggests that there is such a thing as a 'hardy' Type A, who easily withstands the stresses he places on himself. Terry Looker told us that, perhaps, Helen was a hardy type, because 'she looks upon situations as challenging rather than threatening.' Nevertheless, Dr Looker is inclined to the idea that the Type A life is more unproductive than otherwise, and, much more seriously, it is likely to be fatal 'in the long run'. This is because of some of the physiological effects of stress.

Stress

There are two types of stress. One is unavoidable, something which happens to you – the stress of working with noisy machinery, for example, or at a speed dictated not by you but by the machine. The stress of torture is of the same kind. Your body reacts to the pressure or the threat by bringing you to a state of permanent *readiness*. But since you are helpless in the face of the constantly renewed threat your response is never completely discharged. The result is physiological frustration.

The second type of stress is self-induced. If you look for threats and create challenges, you stimulate your own readiness-states. These may or may not be discharged, depending on whether the threat is real or the response is carried out. Type A people are obviously in a permanently charged-up state, and their behaviour suggests that this is never discharged, if only because a further threat or challenge is always looming up over the shoulder of the last.

The physiological state of readiness is primarily the work of the adrenal glands, which are triggered by the brain into producing the hormone adrenaline. This is a natural drug, whose release we experience as 'butterflies'. It has a number of effects, all to do with increasing arousal. It is a stimulant to the heart and the breathing, it causes the liver to shoot glucose into the blood to optimise energy, while the spleen increases its output of oxygen-carrying red blood cells. Adrenaline causes a state of high arousal in advance of the action; it is a 'buzz'.

But for every high there is a low, or at least a feeling of returning equilibrium. These are complex biochemical processes and far from fully understood, but they depend on the release of a variety of hormones and other substances into the bloodstream and at the nerve endings. Chemical changes triggered by excitement and danger can become addictive (just as endorphin release can) and is this which makes activities like gambling, burglary and rock-climbing compulsive. It would also account for the way in which some people become addicted to types of work where excitement is at a premium.

The stress response has to be seen as a useful one since it has obvious survival value. But beyond even that it enhances the quality of life. Without the excitement of anticipated action much of existence would be dull, and the biochemistry of the stress response is part of that excitement. Unfortunately, there are dangers, as Peter's heart attack showed.

Because it causes constriction of blood vessels and a faster heart-rate, the 'fight or flight' response raises blood pressure. In addition, stress detaches cholesterol fat from the stomach lining and releases it into the bloodstream. From all that is known about the chemistry of the blood and the causes of heart disease, this combination of hypertension and cholesterol ought to be catastrophic for the heart and this supposition has been found to be true.

Friedman and Rosenman, the inventors of the Type A classification, studied 1,500 men, both Type A and Type B, and found that heart disease was *twice* as common in the Type As. Their finding has since been confirmed many times over. In addition, Type A behaviour probably also predisposes people to strokes – blood clots which block the flow of blood into the brain, often causing paralysis if not death. People with heart disease are much more likely to suffer strokes, while high blood pressure is also one of the most prominent independent causes of stroke. The significance of this relationship between Type A behaviour on the one hand and heart disease and strokes on the other is that, between them, these diseases account for *more than half of all premature deaths in this country*.

The Social Problems of the Workaholic

The organic health problems of being a workaholic accumulate slowly and unobtrusively. Then they hit you with a bang and you end up like Peter, propped up in a hospital bed wondering 'Why me?' However, compulsive workers subject themselves to a whole set of social problems as well, into which they probably have no more insight than into their furred-up arteries.

We have repeatedly found in discussing compulsions that it is *other people* who bear the first brunt of the problems. In the advanced workaholic there is the same pattern. Unlike drugs and eating disorders, but like alcohol abuse, this is a compulsion which gets worse as you get older. So it is typically marriage partners (rather than, say, parents) who suffer.

History does not record the feelings of the compulsive lunch-liquidiser's wife. But one wife, Gillian, told us what happened to her.

Gillian's Story

Gillian met Colin some fourteen years ago. She was then in her mid-twenties, married with two small children. Dominant and ambitious, with the confidence of a man 'going places', Colin seemed the answer to the boredom and suffocation of her marriage. She left her husband and children and went to live with him.

When they first lived together, Colin ran a retail business selling hardware, household goods and toys. He worked long hours, and would often return home at midnight, tired, dirty and demanding a meal. Gillian had a good job as secretary at a television station, but Colin badgered her into giving this up to join him in the business. From the beginning of their relationship it was clear that Colin had set himself a definite career goal – to do bigger and better things than his successful father. But only gradually did Gillian realise the depth of his work compulsion.

He insisted that she work by his side all the hours humanly

possible. When she was nine months pregnant she was loading and unloading container lorries, and just three weeks after the birth of their daughter he made her travel hundreds of miles to help run his stand at an Earl's Court exhibition. Colin always had several ventures in hand at any one time: Gillian scrubbed floors, filled shelves, hired and fired staff. Staff were always a problem because Colin was such a relentless task master. He would become unbearably irritated if anyone wanted to stop work for lunch, and he never sanctioned tea or coffee breaks.

After ten years, the family moved to a house in Surrey. Colin seemed to be going from strength to strength. He had been among the first people to realise the potential of surf-boards, and he now began importing boards and selling surf-boarding holidays. He owned his own yachts and houses abroad – all the trimmings of business success. So when he persuaded Gillian to raise a loan against her share of the house to ease his cash-flow problems she agreed. Twelve months later Colin left her. Six months after that the bank wrote to say he had failed to keep up the mortgage payments. Today she is virtually penniless and about to become homeless.

Gillian is understandably bitter about Colin's treatment of her and her daughter over the years. 'But also I now realise what a sick person he is. He tried to involve me in his work, but he was never satisfied. When I worked until I dropped, it was still not enough. He tried to persuade me that we were working "for us", but all I was doing was feeding his addiction.'

She now describes life with Colin as 'absolute hell. We never went out. He had no other interests, and we had no social life. He's the only man I've ever known who doesn't need anyone in his life. He doesn't have any friends because you need time to make friends. He hated weekends and would usually go to the office. When he came home at night the office telephone used to be switched through. We did go on holiday once or twice, but he'd phone the office every day.'

Meanwhile Colin missed 'nearly all my daughter's growing up, never attended any school functions, was hardly aware of the little things she was doing'. Today, living alone with no dependants to waste his time, Colin is in his element, living at his office and working twenty-four hours a day. He is linked to the world exclusively through his business number for, as Gillian says, 'he doesn't have a personal phone number'. Now they are divorced he is completely alone and completely at one with his work.

Compulsion

How Workaholics Defeat Themselves

Terry Looker believes that, paradoxically, the Type A workaholic approach is a less productive and less creative way of working. Why should this be? Earlier we sketched out the four main reasons why we get satisfaction from work (see page 81). If we compare this list with Colin's life, we can see how, in him, they have become perverted.

(1) Work does not merely give him a framework for his other activities, it displaces all other activities.

(2) It cuts him off from other people, narrowing not increasing his social horizons.

(3) As he cannot tolerate the slower pace at which other people work, he is hopeless at collective effort. He cannot get satisfaction out of anything which he has not done by himself.

(4) Far from launching his security, identity and confidence, work becomes a bunker in which his essentially weak self-esteem cowers from imagined threats.

Other Ways to Cope

We have now seen the elements of the workaholic syndrome. Through upbringing, learning and conditioning, most of us have some degree of compulsion to work, but certain *types* (Type As) will more often take up extreme compulsive work to cope with their problems. Such problems are exactly the kind of pressures and difficulties we have found underlying other compulsions: Colin, for instance, has been seen (briefly) by two different psychiatrists and, according to Gillian, they both diagnosed him as 'an emotional cripple'. He uses work to feed his aggressive and competitive instincts, and to mask himself off from the rest of reality. At an emotional level he does not function at all.

Once in the grip of the compulsion, it creates its own cycles of problems, and these can make it self-perpetuating. First, you get a 'high' from stress, and may eventually become dependent on it. And second – though your compulsion may start as selfless and principled hard work – it easily degenerates into disregard for the interests of others, and leaves you isolated and unfit for happiness.

So how can you break out of the cycle of compulsive working and slow down? Most people would prefer less drastic strategies to those of a coronary or cerebral thrombosis. But some coronary sufferers end by being paradoxically grateful for their attacks, finding their lives have been forcibly bent in a beneficial direction by the illness. The trouble is the individual's behaviour patterns are so deeply rooted that even after a coronary like Peter's, the effort to change is very often a large one.

Dr Desmond Kelly is medical director of a private psychiatric nursing home which accepts patients on referral from their family doctors. Dr Kelly is also President of the International Stress and Tension Control Society. He sees people of all ages suffering from stress – young people approaching important exams, women in conflict between family and careers and men in middle age facing mounting financial burdens. For him the most difficult to help are the ones who do not realise they need it, 'those who feel that they're indestructible, who cannot see the amber warning light, who are totally addicted to challenge'.

Dr Kelly puts stress patients through a programme which he believes can defuse the most destructive elements of their stress-response. He told us 'One of the most important things is for them to get rid of anger, by taking exercise. That is a great way of burning up adrenaline. Then they need to learn a relaxation technique, either by using a tape, biofeedback, transcendental meditation, yoga, auto-hypnosis or whatever. They also need to take holidays, to say "no" - and they need, almost above all, to be able to sleep.'

A key idea of Dr Kelly's is that stressed people should become realistic in their aims, should lower their sights and 'dare to be average'. Perfection, he maintains, is a snare and delusion. The harder you strive towards it, the further you fall short of it. Since perfection does not exist, perfectionists are guaranteed to be among life's ultimate losers. Being 'average' is a delusion too, of course, but 'it's a benign deception, like a slot-machine that pays £1.50 for every pound you put into it, so it makes you rich on all levels. Just try lowering your standards a little bit. There's nothing worse for a child than to be always given a target a little bit greater than it's able to achieve, because it is then constantly failing. I try to teach people to go for something a little bit lower than a perfect score, like 80 per cent, that'll do. And if they achieve that, they will then feel good. Most of us try to be perfect so we can get ahead in life. But if you lower your sights, you'll hit the target more often.'

Dr Kelly's philosophy – for that is what it amounts to – runs counter to the 'try-try-try again' school of effort. Its drawback is that it is extremely hard to persuade people to abandon beliefs they have held for the best part of a lifetime, and probably learned at their parents' knees. Experiencing a major shock or illness is perhaps one of the few ways in which such attitudes can be shifted. This is certainly what happened to Peter.

Peter Again

After his coronary Peter and Pat were surprised to find no post-coronary care programme available in their area. When they asked the simple question – 'What do we do now?' – the answers they received from hospital and family doctor were scanty. The doctor was himself a running fanatic, and told Peter simply to run. This he did religiously, three miles morning and night. He hated it, and after a year gave up.

Three months after hospital Peter went back to work. But very soon he began to feel deeply stressed, and would be taken home. The stress which he had once thrived on was now threatening to kill him and he had no idea how to deal with it. He followed the well-known prescriptions – he changed to a low-fat diet, he stopped smoking – but these did nothing to prevent his exaggerated reaction to stress.

Then Pat saw a newspaper article describing Terry Looker's anti-stress courses (the Recurrent Coronary Prevention Project) at Manchester Polytechnic. Peter joined the course. Dr Looker told us how he approaches the problem. 'The counselling programme we offer teaches people to modify their perceptions. It was Peter's perception of his work that was his problem – as if it was something threatening to him, and yet it was inside him. So we taught Peter how to change his perceptions, beliefs and habits – a gradual process.'

When you see how Dr Looker operates you realise you are dealing with a process almost identical to parts of the heroin addict's detoxification programme, the modified behavioural therapy for anorexics and bulimics, the self-help groups for those dependent on tranquillisers. The Looker scheme offers a full year of group-work and individual counselling which aims first to *understand* the habits of thought which burden people with a short-fused temper, chronic urgency and irritation at trivialities. Looker's patients learn to pace themselves better, and to accept that some things about oneself are impossible to change, while others *can* be modified. Peter told us:

I don't want to change my personality, but I did need to change my behaviour *patterns*. Now I itemise everything I can do and try to be phlegmatic about the things I can't. I build a waiting-time into every plan of action, and I try to do things one at a time. I think also I now have a more philosophical attitude to the frailty of human nature. It has taken a great deal of mental effort to adopt this approach – to tell someone to ring back, to divert your phone calls to someone else for a bit. Terry's course has allowed me to plan my life. I no longer take my work home, and the drive home is a time to unwind. Perhaps the good thing about having a coronary at the age of forty-two is that you can learn from your mistakes. It's not too late.

Prevention

With previous compulsions we have argued that they can be partly prevented by reducing the availability of the compulsive agent – alcohol, heroin, tranquillisers. As it happens, there has been a large-scale reduction in the amount of available work in the United Kingdom over the last eight years. But paradoxically this has probably tended to increase rather than decrease the degree of stress in the population. For Type A people in particular, unemployment is even more stressful than working too hard. So obviously, the answer to this compulsion will not be found through the abolition of work!

Ideas about combatting the worst ravages of Type A behaviour have largely centred on ways to prevent heart disease, which is still the largest killer in the Western world. Heart disease has been the greatest epidemic of the century. It peaked in the United States in the late 1960s, since when it has declined. In Britain, deaths from heart disease have only much more recently started to fall, and the epidemic is still close to its peak of destructiveness. How much the improved American picture is due to a better diet, more interest in exercise or a more 'laid back' approach to life is debatable. It may be some other factor entirely. Nevertheless, stress reduction has now become part of the orthodoxy of health education, along with dietary change and exercise, regarded as good for the nation in the long term.

Stress Management at Work

Dr Malcolm Carruthers provides a service to industry which aims to reduce the dangers of stress in the workplace. This, he emphasises, is not just because good mental health is worthwhile in itself, but because it makes work more efficient and therefore more profitable. Employees suffering from a build-up of stress are not only prone to sudden collapse, but their judgement can be impaired. Gillian would confirm this: Colin, who was essentially an astute business man, made increasingly incautious decisions towards the end of their marriage, culminating in the debts which have led to the loss of the family home.

Dr Carruthers' main tool is a test which he calls Chemofeedback: an early warning system for stress, heart disease, high blood pressure, strokes, tension and depression. A pin-prick of blood from each employee is analysed to detect cholesterol, clotting factors and other hormones which may underlie depression and tension. This is combined with the blood pressure and a simple psychological video quiz to determine the individual's stress profile which enables Dr Carruthers to recommend how a company can become more efficient. He is fond of comparing his work with that of an accountant. 'Commercial companies are used to people auditing their books, so what we do are *stress audits*, to see whether people are overspent on their energy account. It can all be done on the spot so that within three-quarters of an hour they can have an overall view of whether their stress account is in balance or overdrawn and, if so, what they can do about it.'

This kind of early warning device is helpful, but large-scale prevention of the compulsive problems arising from attitudes to work would be a much larger and more daunting project. It is not even clear if national or government action is effective or desirable. To exhort the people to become ever more competitive and productive on the one hand, while trying to encourage relaxation on the other seems like a paralysing contradiction. The much faster pace of life in our electronic global village makes it even less likely that this circle can be squared. Following the 'Big Bang' in London's Stock Exchange in 1986 63 per cent of employees in City finance houses said it was important to be or to pretend to be a workaholic. One share dealer said: 'I suppose we find our own way of coping. People drink a lot, I've seen some near-fights break out and people in tears. Sometimes everyone gets unbelievably silly. We tease each other a lot, which is fine if they like you, but it can get vicious. I think that is symptomatic of the strain – people don't have time to put up with colleagues they don't get on with. If you don't fit you probably won't last.'

Control and the Sorceror's Apprentice

Coping strategies like these are attempts at checking and *controlling* workaholic behaviour. We tend to think of compulsive behaviour in general as behaviour that is 'out of control'. At the deepest levels of work obsessions, alcoholism and drugs, it is true that reason and judgement have been abandoned and the horse rides the man. Yet underneath the issue of control always lurks. The heroin user invariably believes he can control the drug; the unadmitted alcoholic thinks he can hitch a ride 'on the wagon' anytime; the workaholic asks, with Colin , 'where's the shame in hard work? It's not out of control, it *is* control.'

The Sorceror's Apprentice is a fable which every workaholic should ponder on. In Disney's version we see the young Apprentice left alone by his Master to do some household chores. He soon starts to wonder how he can get the work done more efficiently. In a flash of what he thinks is inspiration he reaches down the Sorceror's Spell Book and, with magic commands, orders the broom to carry out his work for him – to sweep the floors and then to carry water in from the well. Everything goes without a hitch and the Apprentice is even able to speed up the work by multiplying the number of brooms. But then, to his dismay, he realises he does not know how to stop the magic. His dream of finishing the work so quickly and so successfully that the Sorceror will praise him turns into a nightmare, as the broom multiplies into tens and hundreds of brooms, emptying bucket after bucket of water, until the entire house is awash. Only the timely reappearance of the Sorceror saves him from drowning.

So the workaholic who believes he is exercising supreme control has probably not yet looked up the magic words for *stopping* the compulsion. Many who do will find a missing page in the Spell Book – and they cannot always rely on the Sorceror to return home in time.

Chapter 6

Loving Compulsively

I get no kicks from champagne ...
Some get a kick from cocaine ...
But I get a kick out of you. *Cole Porter*

In many human relationships, especially sexual ones, love and
jealousy are intertwined like wrestlers; they struggle for domination,
yet neither has meaning without the other.

The *compulsions* of love and jealousy arise from the anxieties
caused by unbalanced love. We have no difficulty with the idea of
compulsive love. It is much easier to recognise love as a compulsion
than work; much safer and more acceptable for a lover to admit his
dependency than for a drinker, gambler or heroin addict. Nevertheless these states can in some people lead to a living hell as terrible
as the worst heroin withdrawal and as destructive as the most violent
drinking bout.

Eros

Sometimes the darts of love flash to their targets with the uncanny
accuracy of heat-seeking missiles, even under unlikely
circumstances. The physical signs which we have seen again and
again in compulsions are plentiful in the person who is in love. In
fact it is quite conventional to picture Cupid's arrowheads as having
been dipped in some violent nerve-poison, to madden those whom
they puncture. Certainly, the experience of love can be as physiological as a shot of adrenaline, if not quite as deadly as curare.

Bradley Pearson, the middle-aged narrator of Iris Murdoch's
novel *The Black Prince*, falls in love with a girl half his age. He is
alone in his flat when it hits him.

It was a blow, I was felled by it physically. I felt as if my stomach
had been shot away, leaving a gaping hole. My knees dissolved,
I could not stand up, I shuddered and trembled all over, my teeth

chattered. My face felt as if it had become waxen ... I lay there with my nose stuck into the black wool of the rug and the toes of my shoes making little ellipses as I shook with possession. Of course I was sexually excited, but what I felt transcended mere lust to such a degree that although I could vividly sense my afflicted body I also felt totally alienated and changed...

For Pearson, poleaxed and ridiculous but *happy*, the first rush of love transforms everything, like a dose of some psycho-active drug. It charges the brain and changes the perceptions. Every problem is solved or dissolved. Everything becomes simple and explicable. As we saw in the case of Lena, the heroin addict feels exactly the same about junk.

Freud described love from a clinical viewpoint as a brief psychotic episode which cures itself spontaneously. The idea of love as madness is familiar enough in poetry. This is Shakespeare:

Lovers and madmen have such seething brains,
Such shaping fantasies, that apprehend
More than cool reason ever comprehends.

The classic physical symptoms of being in love are very like a withdrawal (or anxiety) state – the dry mouth, the racing heart, the sweating palm; trembling, insomnia, loss of appetite, inattentiveness. But is the 'madness' of love a compulsive state comparable to a drug addiction? One love addict who told us about her experience, Antonia, is in no doubt that it is.

Antonia's Story

'I wouldn't call it a madness. In my case it was much more like an addiction, in the sense that I only felt normal, I only felt happy while I was in the presence of the man concerned, and shortly after leaving him I would still feel all right. I used to say to myself endlessly "Everything's going to be all right", but the longer the intervals between seeing him, the more I felt that gnawing desperation of wondering when I was going to get another fix.

'But unlike other addictions – where you can at least have a swig from the whisky bottle or whatever – whether I saw him or not was entirely dependent on whether he rang me up. I almost never dared to ring him and suggest that we should meet. So I was absolutely at his whim, and sometimes it would be a week, and sometimes ten days, or two weeks. He would never tell me if he was going to be away, or if he was going to be busy. I just had to wait for the next random fix.

'This lasted for nearly two years, and it was a desperate time of my life. But in a sense it *was* a very creative time. It was certainly a time of enormous energy, except that all this energy was one-way, all going from me into him – into thinking about him, into planning what I would say to amuse or entertain him, into planning what I would wear. I very often went out to buy clothes specially to please him, since I felt that my own wardrobe was inadequate to do that.'

Antonia's intense account of her compulsion is striking in two ways. It tells us just what the compulsion was – to be near to this man as often as possible, and to be attractive to him. But it also defines for us the very clear limits of the compulsion: each 'fix' has to be at his invitation, and on his terms. Antonia felt as if she had no rights and no will in the matter, and that she did not control the compulsion – he did. Perhaps this was an important safeguard, since she must have known that he did not love her, and that, if she were to give the compulsion its head and pursue him relentlessly, he would very soon refuse to see her at all.

Even at its most irrational, the behaviour of the compulsive person retains whatever level of control is needed to perpetuate it. The workaholic must be near enough to the ground to raise loans, negotiate contracts, answer letters sensibly, the alcoholic and the junkie have to be well-organised enough to obtain supplies.

Fools of Love

William Hazlitt was a nineteenth-century essayist and friend of the poet Wordsworth. In middle age he fell in love with the much younger Sarah Walker, the daughter of his landlord. This love was as frenzied as it was unrequited. Hazlitt was besotted, experiencing the heights of bliss and the lowest depths of misery in rapid sucession, several times a day. In his account of this infatuation which (like Antonia's) lasted two years, Hazlitt wrote: 'In her sight there was Elysium; her smile was heaven; her voice was enchantment; the air of love waved round her, breathing balm into my heart: for a little while I had sat with the Gods at their golden tables, I had tasted of all earth's bliss … But now Paradise barred its doors against me; I was driven from her presence, where rosy blushes and delicious sighs and all soft wishes dwelt, the outcast of nature and the scoff of love!'

Loving Compulsively

Like a whipped dog, the wretched Hazlitt slinks away. But soon he is asking his friend 'What is to be done? I cannot forget *her*, and I can find no other like what she *seemed*. I should wish you to call, if you can make an excuse, and see whether or no she is quite marble – whether I may go back again at my return, and whether she will see me and talk to me sometimes as an old friend…' As with many of the worst compulsions, one of the first casualties is the pride.

Hazlitt knew he was a Fool of Love, though he could do nothing about it. Jane is another.

Jane's Story

Jane Kelly is a journalist in her early thirties. She admits to falling compulsively in love with men, often men whom she hardly knows and in the most unlikely of places. Writing in the *Mail on Sunday* Jane described how she was 'mugged' by love one day while on a two-week assignment in Reykjavik, capital of Iceland. 'I met him, the love object, eating dried fish at a bus stop. As I stood next to him I had the strongest, strangest feeling that I'd known him before. By the time the bus came I was suffused with desire.'

Reykjavik, although a capital city, is a small town. By the next day, Jane had found out where this young man lived, which was at his parents' house. Her compulsion made her do things she would never normally dream of. She went to the address and, although he was out for the evening, 'I invited myself to dinner. His parents rather reluctantly entertained me. All I wanted was to be close to someone who knew him.'

For the rest of her time in his country, Jane flung herself passionately at the young man. But eventually she had to return to London. Then her withdrawal symptoms began. 'I felt like a heroin addict deprived of a fix. Shaking uncontrollably and unable to eat or sleep. All I could think of was our ten libidinous days rolling in the Icelandic snows. I phoned him every day at 60 pence a minute, and as I heard the interest in his voice fade, the more I had to say.'

Telling

The state of unrequited love is a personal and intimate kind of torture. It is a blocked state of tension, building up in rising steps of intensity, anxiety, fear and hopelessness. There is only one possible release of tension: *telling*. Not all lovers can bear to share

99

their agony with others, though given the right circumstances and encouragement, they find unspeakable relief in doing so. Others, on the other hand, cannot help themselves. They gabble their love to whoever has the patience to listen. At the height of his folly Hazlitt, by his own account, tried his friends – and even perfect strangers – to what must have been the very limits of patience: 'I saw J. going into Will's Coffee-house yesterday morning; he spoke to me. I followed him into the house and whilst he lunched, I told him the whole story. Then I wandered into the Regent's Park, where I met one of Montagu's sons. I walked with him some time, and on his using some civil expression, by God! sir, I told him the whole story. I then went and called on Haydon; but he was out. There was only his man, Sammons, there; but, by God, I could not help myself. It all came out, the whole cursed story! Afterwards I went to look at some lodgings at Pimlico. The landlady at one place, after some explanations as to rent etc, said to me very kindly "I'm afraid you are not well, sir?" – "No, ma'am", said I, "I am not well"; and on enquiring further, the devil take me, If I did not let out the whole story, from beginning to end!'

Hazlitt found a final relief, a sort of exorcism, in writing the account of his love for Sarah Walker in a book he called *Liber Amoris* ('The Book of Love'). For a while the book did his reputation as a serious journalist great damage, for it was far too painfully intimate, too naked by half, for the sophisticated tastes of Georgian London. One reviewer called it 'nauseous and revolting. It ought to exclude the author from all decent society', while *The Times* called him 'this impotent sensualist'.

But if your friends will not listen, and you have no literary gift, then you may need to pay a professional listener – a therapist or marriage guidance counsellor.

Is Love an Illness?

As we have seen, Freud's answer was yes, though he thought it an illness which is pointless to treat it since it gets better by itself. Nevertheless the distress and disruption which it may cause is so great that some lovers do undoubtedly appear to need help. Clinical psychologist Paul Brown has written a specialist paper on the 'Disorder of Falling in Love' in which he presents the case of a married couple, whom we shall call John and Sarah.

Loving Compulsively

The Story of John and Sarah

They were in their early forties and had been married for twenty-one years. They had children aged eighteen and twenty who were both at university. John was a banker; Sarah did not work outside the home.

One morning Sarah returned to the house from shopping to find a note from John. It told her that their marriage was over and he had left home to live in a flat he had rented some five miles away. He would be living with a woman with whom he had fallen in love. He said he was very happy, and could they meet soon to discuss money. He hoped she could forgive him.

When they met as arranged in a pub, Sarah found John in a state of high excitement. He seemed quite incapable of considering her or their children's feelings in the matter, and was anxious only to get the financial settlement over with as quickly as possible. He made a number of quite unrealistically generous promises about money, and then hurried away, driven by his girlfriend who had been waiting in the car.

Sarah went to see Dr Brown, who then made arrangements for John to visit him. At first he was defensive, but then broke down in tears. He said he had lost all control of his feelings over the past six weeks, since he realised he loved (and was loved by) a new colleague at work. He felt he had no choice but to do what he did, as the compulsion to be with her had been so strong. But this was against his rational judgement, and he was deeply distressed about the pain he was causing Sarah and the children.

John's sense of being divided between two strong sets of feelings continued, as was obvious from his behaviour. Over the next ten days he returned to his wife twice and left her again twice. After each return John and Sarah had made love - the first time in such a way that she took it as a reaffirmation of their relationship. The second time, their love-making had had a quality of desperation which she found frightening. The existence of the other woman was not mentioned between them on either occasion.

Dr Brown comments that both John and Sarah had become detached from reality by their unnerving experience, and that the therapist needs to try to *re*attach them. He should try to determine whether the marriage has really broken down, but should not 'take sides'.

Dr Brown speculates that the compulsive lover's sudden and inappropriate behaviour comes about when the human need for intimate expression is slowly buried alive amid the humdrum business of living. Any long-established marriage (however loving) can settle into a pattern where the partners communication is reduced to short-hand. They know each other so well that they no longer need to show their feelings openly. But if, perhaps in middle age, either partner should meet 'a new source of intimacy' this can take them so by surprise that they become overwhelmed. They are like ex-addicts who have lost their tolerance for a drug. Any large dose knocks them off their feet.

What overwhelms them is an all-engulfing high, the ecstatic happiness of first love discovered all over again. But unlike *first* love, this experience also involves inevitable feelings of 'existential depression'. The new love demands the abandonment of all old ways. Like fresh paint it covers the old life. But there are feelings of guilt, panic and anxiety over what must be painted over and lost, if the compulsion is to be followed to the end. Under these circumstances, says Dr Brown, it is unlikely that the usual anti-depressant drugs will be much use. The experience of love itself probably prompts the release of endorphins in the brain, which in his view are the reason for the euphoria of lovers such as Hazlitt and the fictional Bradley Pearson. This endorphin release is inevitably followed by 'down' periods which are not counteracted by conventional anti-depressants.

Jane and Antonia know the toll that this capacity to fall unexpectedly and almost insanely in love takes on their lives, and would like to cure themselves if they could. Antonia told us of her attempts to cure herself of her most recent emotional addiction 'partly by analysing it *as* an addiction and therefore realising that it was an unnatural thing, and a bad thing. Like most addicts I suppose I did suffer terribly. I mean I felt myself to be in real pain. The blood was invisible, but the pain was real enough. It distorted the rest of my life, it distorted my relationships with my friends, my children, at work. I couldn't really do anything except concentrate on this man, and I realise it was completely irrational.

'I did actually try to end the relationship after a year. It's a curious thing that in that first year, although I moved house so as to be closer to him, I never told him I loved him. It's as though, somehow, that was the last bastion of pride – I could *keep* that. Obviously he knew, everybody knew, but I never actually articulated it. So, finally I wrote him a letter, which I deliberately posted on the day I was going on holiday for a fortnight away from him, to Italy. I knew I'd be happy in Italy, and I knew that I couldn't have immediate second thoughts, so I wrote this letter in which I said "You know, of course, that I love you, but the imbalance between your kindly indifference to me, and my overwhelming love for you, is no longer bearable, and I wish to put a stop to it." And curiously enough he wouldn't let me do it. Now, he never referred to the letter, but as soon as I came back he telephoned me, he asked me round to dinner, he generally behaved as if nothing had happened. And of course my obsession with him was still so great that since he appeared willing to see me I couldn't break it off.'

Shadows in the Upbringing

It took another whole year for Antonia's compulsion to run its course. She is such an articulate witness that we wondered if she had been able to analyse the reasons for her tendency to behave like this. She told us: 'Well I think the people to whom it happens perhaps have this in common, that, as children, they were very much dependent on the approval of the parent of the opposite sex. Now my father was a good man, and probably saw himself as a loving father, but he seemed very remote, very undemonstrative. He didn't love me for being his daughter, I felt, he loved me if I did well. So if I passed exams, or won the approval of his friends, or helped by serving drinks at one of their parties, I would be approved and I would be loved. So I always felt that I was really inadequate, and that I had to try my very, very best to have any hope of being liked by this God-like creature.'

We put this to the psychotherapist Mavis Klein, who commented 'What is most striking to me in what Antonia says is the comparison between the repeated pattern in her adult relationships and the pattern that she herself so precisely describes from her childhood. What I encounter time and time again amongst people, especially in their love relationships, is an overt quest to achieve the opposite of the pains that they experienced as children. Yet, with the precision and subtlety that the unconscious mind is capable of we always, in fact, end up choosing the same painful patterns, again and again and again.'

The politician's maxim 'Those who cannot learn from history are condemned to repeat it' has its echo, then, in the personal and psychic history of the individual. At some point in their upbringing, children in this culture come across two compelling ideas about romance and adult relationships. The first of these is that our relationships with our parents are rehearsals for future adult attachments, and the second suggests that compulsive love is the finest and most important expression of these adult relationships. Both are fantasies, although marvellous ones. They are also contradictory, creating an emotional puzzle that makes potential Antonias, Janes, Johns, Hazlitts and Bradley Pearsons out of all of us.

Loss

The teacher and writer C. S. Lewis had been a life-long bachelor, living for many years in adulthood as a sort of grown-up boy, sharing house with his brother, also unmarried, in the almost exclusively masculine world of Oxford University. Suddenly, in his middle age, a woman came uninvited into his life, a Jewish American divorcee named Joy who was compounded, it seemed to Lewis, of strangeness heaped on strangeness. And so strange were his emotions that, even when Lewis secretly married Joy, he pretended that it was not for love but as a convenience, purely to enable her to stay in Britain as a resident. Only later, when she became suddenly ill with cancer, was Lewis forced to acknowledge that he loved her.

This love shocked Lewis's friends, not because there was anything improper in it, but because it seemed so utterly improbable. For a few years Joy – a pun he made himself – utterly filled and changed his life. When she died from her illness, he documented his reaction in *A Grief Observed*.

> No one ever told me that grief felt so like fear. I am not afraid, but the sensation is like being afraid. The same fluttering in the stomach, the same restlessness, the yawning. I keep on swallowing.

Once again we come across these physiological reactions. Love makes you feel wonderful, the loss of love makes you ill. There is now conclusive evidence that grief damages the body's immune system, so that recently bereaved people have a higher risk of death in the first six-to-nine months after the death of the spouse. Then the mind and body adjust to the new conditions, and the death-rate returns to the national average.

Love and Conflict

If the sudden and unexpected bliss of love is like a drug – the effects

of hormones and endorphins released in the brain and other organs
– then one thing that is sure is that it will gradually create tolerance.
The intensity of the mind and body's reactions dwindles, as with
any drug. So far this entirely accords with human experience. But
with drug addiction the loss of pleasure does not mean a loss of
addiction; so also with love. You remain in love but at a lower level
of pleasure intensity, while continuing to enjoy the occasional *rush*
of more intense feeling from time to time. This too is in line with
our common experience of what happens in long-term loving
relationships.

Some compulsive lovers are able to maintain the level of pleasure,
though this is nearly always at the cost of great accompanying
insecurity. Antonia's description shows that, by allowing herself to
be an entirely passive lover, she ensured that her 'doses' of love were
unpredictable and insufficient. Her passivity was her insurance
against 'tolerance' and the lessening of the intensity of her love. It
also had another use. Antonia knew her love was entirely one-sided,
and also that one-sided lovers, if out of control, inevitably destroy
their relationship with their love object. One businessman we heard
of phoned his girlfriend ninety times a day. Another had something
similar happen to him. He ended a relationship with a woman, but
whenever he arrived at the station on his way to work, he would find
her waiting for him. He always brushed past her onto the platform,
but on arrival at the destination, he would find she had taken a taxi,
and was waiting for him there too. No one can stand this kind of
unnerving pressure for long. You either face a nervous breakdown
or call the police, as Susan found.

Susan's Story

Susan was a twenty-four-year-old secretary, leading a normal,
independent social life and living with her parents. She met a boy
at a party and they went out together casually for a month or so.
Susan did not intend to become emotionally involved: as far as
she was concerned they were never more than friends. But a
frightening gap had opened up between their two perceptions of
the relationship. The casual friendship had turned, for him, into
an all-consuming passion. From now on Susan became the object
of reckless and relentless pursuit: 'He used to paint "I love you
Susie" in lipstick on my car. He painted the same thing all over
his car and used to drive in front of me. He kept ringing me at
home, and then coming round to the house at all hours. I had to

go to the doctor to get tranquillisers. At last my father got his solicitor involved, but in spite of warning letters, he wouldn't stop. So we took him to court, and he refused to agree to leave me alone. Eventually he went to jail for two months, and I have never seen or heard of him again.'

We have already commented on the heroic side of many compulsions. The imprisonment of this anonymous lover is in the same class.

The Green-eyed Monster

To fall selflessly in love is to feel as if you have dropped into the hands of another. That person can do what they like with you, and much to your surprise this makes you happy. To love jealously, on the other hand, is to desire to *be the owner yourself*, to have and hold the other person as an exclusive and uncontested proprietor. Selfless or one-sided love is often a kind of martyrdom; jealousy is about power and possession.

Othello is the greatest and most complete exploration of this theme in literature, and Iago's advice to Othello in the play is explicit:

> Oh Beware my Lord of jealousy;
> It is the Green-eyed monster which doth mock
> The meat it feeds on.

So, while love, for all its pangs, is symbolised as a chubby, winged toddler with a bow and arrows, jealousy is a ravenous beast feeding on human flesh. But, of course, we also recognise both emotions as peculiarly human. William Blake warned that

> Cruelty hath a human heart,
> Jealousy a human face.

And as we shall see from Frances's story, jealousy which starts with love, ends in cruelty.

Frances's Story

Frances is in her mid-thirties. When she was twenty-two she married George, who was twelve years older. He had three children by two previous marriages and he and Frances went on to have two more children of their own. It took Frances some time to realise in full why George's two previous marriages had failed.

Initially she was greatly attracted to George's energy and drive. He was a workaholic. He had three separate careers and launched two successful businesses. In one of these Frances worked alongside him, helping to set it up. They employed a nanny to care for the young children while she worked with her husband. But gradually she began to realise that his insistence that they work together was a by-product of his intense possessiveness. Frances tried to respond to this at first with sympathy: she saw herself as the one who would help him to work it out.

But instead of diminishing, George's jealousy simply grew, feeding on itself. When she was not at the office with him, George would leave her long lists of jobs to do, using these as an excuse to phone her – sometimes ten times in a day – to see if she had completed them. After the birth of their second son, Frances felt under a lot of stress, and it was at this time that George began to insist on taking all incoming telephone calls himself, on the pretext that she was not well enough. Gradually this pattern was established, and George increasingly hated Frances using the telephone.

She had to endure increasingly intense daily interrogations about where she had been, who she had seen and spoken to. He also felt it necessary to cross-question the nannies about what Frances had been doing, so that any nanny who became too friendly with Frances would be dismissed on the grounds that she could not be trusted to give true answers.

Frances's family were kept away from the house on various pretexts, and she was allowed no social life. People were rarely invited to the house, and then never more than once. Anyone she said she liked was criticised and abused – one female friend was even accused of wanting to have a lesbian relationship with her George would frequently take her car keys, pretending that her car needed mending and was unsafe to drive. She would be marooned in the house for days at a time, more than a mile from the nearest village.

At the end of their relationship, George had begun to make explicit accusations of sexual infidelity. For the first time he was becoming physically violent, and she became frightened for her safety. Jealousy is probably the most common motive for assaults between sexual partners, and Frances's fears seemed amply justified when the full extent of George's monitoring activities were revealed. One day she found a filing cabinet in his office which contained a complete file on her going back to the beginning of their marriage. It contained tape recordings of her telephone calls, photographs, logs of her movements, receipts for purchases and car mileages. She was amazed and disconcerted to find similar files on his two previous wives.

Jealousy, by a distorted logic of its own becomes the dark accompanyist of love. Love is supposed to be perfect union between two people, but this ideal is of necessity unattainable. As realisation of this dawns on the jealous person, the jealous passion is fed by it. That is why Iris Murdoch's Bradley Pearson, struck down with impotent jealousy, describes jealousy as 'a sort of exercise or play of the reason'. It is reason picking out the flaws in desire.

In the absence of the perfect romantic unity, possessive lovers are compelled to exist in a chronic state of agony. They are tortured by the inability really to know the objects of their love. If you cannot know them you cannot know if, on any given occasion, they are telling the truth. And if you suspect they might *once* lie, then why should they not lie more often? Why not all the time? To Othello, in the deepest throes of his jealousy, the guiltless Desdemona becomes 'A closet, lock and key of villainous secrets'.

Before long jealousy becomes a special kind of paranoia, in which the world attacks you through your loved one. Then the jealous state becomes the negative image of the loving state. Like love, it completely fills the future, though with pain rather than happiness. When Bradley Pearson experiences jealousy this is exactly how he feels it: 'It was not simply that I frenziedly desired what I could not have. That was but a blunt and unrefined kind of suffering. I was condemned to be *with* her even in her rejection of me. And how long, and how slow, and how drawn-out that rejection would be ... I had acquired a dimension of suffering which would poison and devour my whole being, as far as I could see, for ever.'

So the jealous person realises full well that he can never know his loved one as he knows himself. But this does not mean he does not try. George's efforts to keep tabs on Frances would have done credit to a private investigator. In the novel *The End of the Affair* Graham Greene portrays a jealous man having an affair with his friend's wife. But it is the lover, not the husband, who hires a private detective, suspecting her of having a second affair. The details he finds out about her life – the diary he obtains – bring him enlightenment and a sense of power, but no happiness. The jealous person's compulsion is not pursued in the name of happiness, but of power.

We have looked at jealousy from the point of view of the victim of the process, the innocently accused, besieged wife. Philip shared with us his experience as a man whose own unreasonable jealousy drove him to destroy his marriage.

Philip's Story

Like George, Philip has been married three times. His first wife was nineteen and he was twenty-two; it lasted sixteen months. His second attempt, four years later, was in duration more successful and lasted four years. He met his third wife Tracy while still married and running a pub. Tracy was herself married with three children, but unhappy.

From the start Philip felt a great desire to be the *protector* of Tracy and her children, and after the birth of their own son this feeling became even stronger. With two failures behind him, he desperately wanted this marriage to succeed. Perhaps this was the reason for his growing obsession with staying near Tracy as much as possible. He began inventing excuses at work to leave early in order to go home. But it was more than this: he wanted her *all to himself.* He found it increasingly difficult to tolerate visitors at weekends, not even Tracy's family. Visits by her sister, with whom Tracy was very close, were discouraged.

Philip was naturally dismayed when Tracy insisted on going out to work, though he had no option but to agree. However, it made the torment of his jealousy even keener, for it meant she would now come into contact with managers, reps, warehouse staff – *men.*

Inevitably he began to accuse her of having affairs with these men. Then, as the compulsion grew, he started drinking. They decided to go to a marriage guidance counsellor. 'We attended, oh, ten or eleven sessions, and we didn't seem to be making any progress at all and then, after a while, things seemed to be looking up, and we seemed to be getting on better at home. And then, one week, we finally went there and the Marriage Guidance Counsellor asked us how we were, and how had things been in the last week, and my wife turned round and said "Well, Philip's presence around me annoys me." The situation now is that I've been divorced. I've no plans to start another relationship, because I'm still in love with my wife. Or rather my ex-wife.'

Dr Paul Brown finds in Philip's story less an assertion of power than a fear of loss. 'He seemed to be very frightened of his wife being away from him, as if terrified of separation. That feeling, when it becomes morbid, is jealous possession and jealous attachment. The trouble is that this creates no space for the other person.' What follows is exactly the situation in reality that the jealous person has feared in fantasy. Those who are the objects of jealousy – Tracy or Frances – leave. 'They *prove* to themselves that they really will lose the person: then that is the self-fulfilling prophecy. The unconscious psychological processes have won, even though the person on the outside believes they've lost. The battle inside is the destructive one.'

Mavis Klein sees jealousy as a compulsion which turns back against the sufferer. 'My understanding of extreme and pathological jealousy is that it represents very low self-esteem in the person who feels it.' But she believes that there is something to be said for a certain amount of jealousy, as a form of self-criticism. 'Somebody who has never experienced jealousy, whose self-esteem is so high that they have *never* experienced it, lacks a certain modesty and humility, and that is also appropriate to being human.'

Is there Jealousy with Reason?

We have looked at jealousy as an unconscious rejection of a person, as part of a grab for power and possession and as a form of self-punishment. Such are the conflicts and paradoxes of the mind that jealousy may feasibly be some or all of these at the same time. However, such kinds of jealousy will be built on fantasy, they will be 'morbid' or pathological. What about the jealousy you feel when you know that your partner *is* being unfaithful? Is it a reasonable emotion? Is it useful?

Nancy Friday argues in her book *Jealousy* that jealousy is the glue which sticks a love-triangle together. A triangle of this kind is essentially an arena of conflict. When the triangle eventually breaks apart and the issue is decided, the power of jealousy with which two of the members fight over the third determines the outcome.

The amount of jealousy brought to bear in such a situation varies. Some people are more jealous than others and, according to Nancy Friday, those who suffer most painful losses early on in childhood are the most vulnerable. 'Some people go twenty or thirty years without feeling it again because they've constructed their lives accordingly. They've decided not to care so much again. But if you run away from jealousy you run away from love.'

Loving Compulsively

In the past, triangles of this type, she believes, more often existed between a man and two women, and this meant that jealousy was a peculiarly female problem – women had more *reason* to be jealous. But now she sees signs of a change. Women are sexually freer and more adventurous than they were, and this has led to an increase in triangles with a different power-distribution, that of two men vying for one woman. She may even be supported by the facts. A survey recently suggested that 55 per cent of married women today have affairs.

But we think it is arguable that women have been historically more jealous than men. The history of crime (carried out by men and women) is littered with criminal passions, usually originating in jealousy. A recent survey in Detroit found that 20 per cent of murders (nearly all of which are committed by men) were motivated by jealousy, and there seems little reason in common sense to believe that the proportion of jealous crimes in the past has not always been as high or even higher. Two of our examples of extreme addictive jealousy in this chapter have been men; the two great jealous heroes in Shakespeare – Othello and King Leontes in *A Winter's Tale* – were both men. It may, perhaps, be true that women are *doing* more about jealousy today – they do commit more violent crime than they used to, for instance. But the condition of jealousy seems a universal and even a natural one for both sexes.

We have stated that the problem of compulsion in love and in jealousy is no different in essentials from other compulsive behaviour. They have similar physiological effects, and they provide ample opportunity to escape into disguises and artificial personalities, and also for self-punishment. The explanation of psycho-analysis, first put forward by Freud and developed by his successors in various ways, suggests that the origins of these compulsions are even more firmly rooted in the early childhood than others we have discussed. The general background picture is one of emotional insecurity, low self-esteem and an attempt at finding a solution – a *coping strategy* – for these unhappy feelings. Such behaviour – Freud called it 'repetition- compulsion' – can be thought of as a striving after perfection. And the compulsive lover is above all a perfectionist. Love and jealousy are all-or-nothing affairs.

Where compulsions force the individual into extremes of antisocial behaviour, or of personal danger, then some kind of psychiatric help is obviously called for.

Compulsion

Love, Jealousy and Counselling

The shape of our adult lives is determined by our attitudes to love. Millions of people wade miserably through life because of mistaken beliefs about love; they carry with them as they go the scars of broken marriages, domestic violence and mental cruelty, all sustained in the name of love. In Britain one third of all attempts at tying the marriage knot 'till death do us part' last less than ten years.

More of these relationships would last if they were based on realistic expectations and if the compulsive nature of romantic love and jealousy were better understood. Many people find that a sympathetic counsellor can help unravel some of their behaviour-patterns, and understand the roots of anxiety and stress which make them run round in such destructive circles.

There is no more humane account of love than that of the psychotherapist and writer Erich Fromm. 'Mature love is union under the condition of preserving one's integrity', says Fromm. It requires 'a state of intensity, awakeness, enhanced vitality, which can only be the result of being productive and active in many other spheres of life'. We are then freed to have 'active concern for the life and the growth of the one whom we love'. There could hardly be a better statement of ideal non-compulsive love. It is a love in which destructive jealousy finds little place, while the happiness of personal love, a natural high which is only partly to do with sexual physiology, is not abolished, but enhanced and prolonged.

If, on the other hand, you become too bound up in circular repetitive patterns of love – either in the martyred selflessness of Antonia or the jealous possessiveness of Colin and Philip – you are inevitably and immediately crowded round with anxieties: that the person in whose hands you lie will drop you; that you will lose the person whom you want to possess entirely. Successful love is maintained by balancing competing tensions, like a suspension bridge between possessing and being possessed. The fact that this happens relatively rarely shows the instability of many love relationships, and how precarious are the foundations on which they are built.

Chapter 7

Wider Perspectives

In this book we have looked in some detail at six different forms of compulsive behaviour of varying seriousness. The first four chapters dealt with food and mood-changing drugs, while the last two showed that we may become 'hooked' on work, or even on the emotions of love and jealousy. But the object of compulsion can be almost anything and in this chapter we shall briefly discuss some other very common compulsions, before going on to draw some more general conclusions.

One of the most widespread of compulsions is *gambling*, which is in every way as addictive and as destructive for sufferers and their families as any drug problem. We hear increasingly of people hooked not just on traditional forms of gambling, like betting on horses and dogs, but on electronic machines such as 'Space Invaders' and other video games. Several young men contacted us about their compulsion to spend all their time and money in these amusement arcades: this had led them into stealing and deception, and ruined their chances of passing school exams or finding a job.

Tom's Story

Tom, a fourteen-year-old, told us: 'There's a group of us at school, always hanging around this mini-cab office where they've got a really brilliant machine. It's very realistic. It's based on a fast car on a country road, and you get a higher score depending on how long you can keep on driving fast without crashing. If you've got one of the top ten scores your name is on a sort of roll of honour with your score. I can't keep away. If some other guy's on the machine I get really frustrated and on edge, wanting him to finish so I can have a go. So I bunk off school and go down there on my own sometimes. It's my ambition to be number one, the best, but it costs a lot of money. I have to get it out of my mum's bag sometimes when she's not looking. I don't know, I probably spend twenty or thirty pounds a week on it ...'

113

Compulsion

For some teenagers the thrills of a simulated high-speed car is not enough: they crave the real thing, and in such people *car theft* may develop into a compulsion. These teenagers often plan meticulously, even to the point of only marking down certain makes of car to steal. The euphoric 'high' they feel as they race at high speeds – especially if pursued by the police – is comparable to that of the binge-eater. The intervals between incidents may be filled with depression and restlessness.

This kind of behaviour, like drug-taking, can become epidemic. Recently there was an outbreak of joy-riding by teenagers – and even younger children – in Dublin. At its height scores of cars were being broken into and driven away every night, and the Irish police were devoting more resources to combatting the craze than to any other crime.

Another obviously risky crime is *housebreaking*. For some people burglary is a profession, but it is one that can be peculiarly hard to give up. We know of one family with a weekend cottage which has been broken into four times by the same man over a period of two years. On each visit he cleared the cottage of its furniture until, by the time of his fourth visit, the owners had almost nothing of any value left in the place. Yet the burglar had to make away with something, so he took a set of blackened saucepans. When this burglar was caught he asked for twenty-six other break-ins to be taken into consideration by the court.

Terry's Story

Terry, a compulsive burglar in his forties, told us: 'You get out of prison and you're dead set on never going back there. You promise the wife, "This time I'll go straight" and for a few weeks that's what you do. But then some chance comes up – you meet up with some old mate or something – and in no time at all you find you're planning a new job. I can't really describe the feeling. It's very exciting and very frightening at the same time – you get into this person's house and, you know, your heart's pounding and you're all charged up ready to run at the slightest sound. You get a great kick out of it afterwards, though. It's like a feeling of light-headedness that *I did it, I got away with it*. Then, after a little while, you start getting bored and a bit restless, and then in no time you're planning another job, and it starts all over again. I know the odds are I'll get caught again, eventually, but it's like you can't leave off. You're hooked.'

114

Shoplifting too can become a serious psychological problem, with very complicated reasons behind it. It is certainly an adrenaline 'thrill', but it can also be interpreted in some people as a distress signal. One case of a middle-aged titled woman, once a nationally known television personality, brought this to the public's attention a few years back. She had been widowed and depressed, but she was certainly not poor. Yet she was caught taking a few small items of food from a local shop. Later, some time after magistrates had imposed a fine on her, she was found dead from an overdose of sleeping pills. This tragic case caught the conscience of the public, and has led to the formation of a national network of self-help groups for people convicted of shoplifting.

However it is not just shoplifting, but *shopping* itself which is now beginning to be seen as potentially compulsive. The existence of 'shopaholics' - as they are known in the United States – highlights the fact that almost any activity which we find pleasurable, however normal in other respects, may get out of control. In fact, it was while we were researching the work of a self-help group in New York City, Shopaholics Anonymous, that we had the idea for this book. Two of the stories we heard then illustrate the syndrome.

Liza's Story

Liza is a twenty-eight-year-old black woman, who is divorced and lives with her daughter of ten. She works part time and is on a low income. After her divorce three years ago she became depressed, and started going on shopping binges to alleviate this. 'I'm a compulsive spender, and if I see something I'll buy it, and if I have a credit card I'll use it up to the limit. I would go to a store and buy, buy, buy for myself and my daughter. It made me feel great at the time, it fed my ego and stopped me feeling low. Of course, afterwards, when I realised no way could I pay the bills when they came in, I felt guilty and hated myself.' At that time Liza had thirteen credit cards. Her first act upon joining the shopaholics self-help group was to hand over the credit cards for safe keeping. The group operates a 'buddy system', so that when Liza feels the desire go on a shopping spree, she can telephone another member of the group. The two then talk through the compulsion until it dies away.

Compulsion

Mary's Story

Mary's compulsive shopping followed a similar pattern of depression and anxiety leading to shopping sprees which were then followed by guilt and self-disgust. 'Although I have a reasonable job in advertising, I was spending twice as much as my salary, about 5 thousand dollars a month, mainly on clothes. I would rush through the shops not even trying things on, often buying things I didn't need, just like a shoplifter. But I had fifteen credit cards and the urge was so strong, I never thought about the consequences. By the time I got home I felt so guilty I'd sneak the bags in and hide them in the closet. Often I didn't unwrap them for days. Sometimes friends would come over and buy the clothes from me to help me out. I knew there was something wrong – somehow I was shopping to make myself feel loved, to fill a void that I didn't know how to fill in any other way.' Mary has been having therapy for over a year now and feels much happier. She has also cut her credit cards down from fifteen to three.

Mary's therapist describes compulsive shopping in very similar terms to those of Susie Orbach on anorexia. Although there are male 'shopaholics', the majority are women. Women may have this problem, the therapist believes, if they do not feel in control of their lives and are not brought up as men are to learn to control money. They are also, quite literally, trying to buy love and self-esteem.

This is an American view. In Britain, it used to be a firm working-class tradition that a wife controlled the family finances, since it was she who did the shopping. That tradition does not, however, apply so strongly in the newer suburban areas especially among those who are 'upwardly mobile', and it is here that the boom in credit card ownership has resulted in many people, especially women, getting into serious debt. The famous slogan which was used to launch the Access card told us that it 'takes the waiting out of wanting'. Today the same card is marketed as 'your flexible friend'.

It can be seen how these aspects of compulsive shopping fit in with our previous remarks about compulsions. The credit card is the instrument but not the goal of the compulsion. Its promise of immediate gratification for passing desires, combined with a warm and friendly image, can prove irresistible to people whose lives are in other ways frustrated and friendless. The mask of credit enables compulsive spenders to forget their anxieties with 'trouble-free' shopping, while the lash of debt catches them on the rebound and fills them with remorse and self-punishment.

We have already pointed out the similarity between compulsive shopping and 'binge eating'. Liza told us that she had herself gone through a period of compulsive eating and extreme dieting, and this raises the interesting question of whether people who suffer from one compulsion are more likely to suffer from others.

Cross-compulsion

Many people combine various forms of compulsive behaviour, as we frequently observe in everyday life: the heavy smoker who is also a problem drinker; the compulsive gambler who smokes; the workaholic knocking back gins at the end of the day to try to relax; or the shopaholic like Liza who goes on food binges.

It used to be thought that there was such a thing as a 'compulsive personality type' which explained this tendency towards multiple compulsions. However we believe it is more productive to think of different compulsive behaviour patterns as showing family resemblances to each other. These resemblances are evident both in their effects and in the way in which they originate from underlying social and psychological dilemmas. These similarities mean that compulsions are potentially interchangeable. For example, most compulsions offer a release from anxiety – however temporary – and many give a feeling of control which, as we have seen, is often lacking in the emotional lives of many compulsive people.

So, once compulsions are pictured as attempts, however misguided, to cope with deep seated real life problems, the actual choice of compulsion may be almost a matter of chance. The attempt to 'fill a void' caused by lack of love and self-esteem can be made equally well by 'filling up' with food or drink, buying consumer goods or dreaming about a loved one. It may also be temporarily eased by the desire to walk a tightrope between exhilaration and disaster, to feel that addictive biochemical 'rush' of the danger-response which is common to the rock climber, the burglar, the gambler, the compulsive worker and even the jealous husband.

We believe this explanation for cross-compulsion has far more to offer than the more rigid idea of the compulsive personality, particularly because of what it implies about treatment. A problem in someone's life, however hidden and convoluted, is more accessible and more likely to be changed than a personality trait, whether inborn or acquired.

Compulsion

Nevertheless, it does mean that the *primary life problem* of the compulsive individual must be tackled directly. Unlike the behavioural treatments we have looked at, it will not be appropriate for therapists to concentrate solely on the compulsive behaviour: the underlying causes must be found, or it is all too probable that one pattern of compulsive behaviour will be replaced by another. An ex-heroin addict explained how, after she had given up heroin, she became a compulsive drinker, using alcohol in a similar way to heroin. Now that she has given up drinking she is left with a compulsive eating problem, and finds she cannot control her food intake any more easily than she once controlled drugs and drink. Psychotherapy is at last helping her to begin to understand the more basic distress which has given rise to these uncontrolled appetites.

One interesting discovery has confirmed the importance of the compulsive person's deep-seated primary problems. A study of the different methods of treating alcohol dependency came up with an unexpected result: that *no treatment at all turned out to be as effective as the various patent methods of treatment*. In other words, in many cases, it appeared that the compulsion resolved itself spontaneously. This, however, was not quite the case. The common factor in 'spontaneous' recoveries from alcohol dependence was almost always a major life change – getting married, moving away, becoming a parent. Some of these are quite natural developments in a person's life, to do with getting older and more mature, but their influence nevertheless suggests that we are capable of entirely breaking a troublesome compulsion by 'growing out of it' and changing our lives.

The context is even more important with heroin addiction than with alcohol. We have already seen how the addict tends to live within a particular subculture: when this is removed, the heroin compulsion can also be removed. If the underlying problem is also solved the addict is securely rehabilitated. This was found by the US army following the Vietnam war. Thousands of servicemen had become addicted to heroin during their postings to the war-zone, and the authorities had braced themselves for an enormous escalation of the nation's already daunting heroin problem. This, however, did not happen. 72 per cent of heroin-addicted veterans came off heroin once the context of their addiction – the war – had disappeared.

Counselling

Throughout this book we have emphasised the importance of

understanding the compulsion and of coming to terms with the underlying problems which originally caused the sufferer to 'choose' a compulsive behaviour pattern as a coping strategy. This, of course, can be rather more easily said than done.

We have suggested that *counselling* either with one counsellor (say, a family doctor or trained therapist) or in a group setting (sharing experiences with other sufferers) can provide the insight and support necessary. We have also seen that the problems caused by the compulsion involve not just sufferers but their family and friends. Very often the parents of an anorexic or a drug-user have great difficulty helping their child, and may also feel enormous guilt. As an example of the effect of this, it was found that the most powerful influence over the 28 per cent of heroin-using American troops who *continued* to use the drug after Vietnam was the 'parental attitude'. It seems clear that such families, too, would have benefited from some form of counselling. So what is it, and how does it help?

A good counsellor depends on a relationship of trust with the person who is counselled. The counsellor 'gives permission' for the sufferer to talk about what are often difficult and hidden feelings, some of which may stem from events that took place years before. One tranquilliser user told us of her need to 'tell my story to someone who would understand'. If she had had a sympathetic ear at the outset, she feels, she would have avoided two decades of waste and futility. In this type of situation, listening is the most important therapy there is.

There have been thousands of books devoted to the different aspects of the 'therapeutic relationship', from the psychoanalysis of Freud and his followers to the therapeutic communities and self-help groups we have mentioned. Counselling *does* seem to be essential both in enabling the compulsive person to recognise the problem of the compulsion and to look deeper into the possible causes. Nor is this just a matter of 'talking things through'. Often what comes out is practical help and advice about a specific problem: bad housing, unemployment, problems with children, all difficulties which can lead to compulsion, but which can often be resolved if the person is referred to the right agency. This is where the family doctor *can* play a vital role. But all too often that first moment of contact between doctor and compulsion sufferer turns out to be a disappointment and a missed opportunity.

Compulsion

Is Medicine to Blame?

We have heard a constant refrain about the lack of medical skill –
and sometimes sympathy – in doctors dealing with cases of
compulsive behaviour. Since the general practitioner is the first port
of call for most people in search of help, this is a sad waste. People
have described how doctors simply had no time to talk (or listen)
to them, or else failed to refer them for the kind of help they needed.
We have seen in detail how the regrettably common response of
prescribing tranquillisers has caused much unnecessary suffering for
many. GPs we spoke to were usually aware of this, but only some
put it down to their lack of training in psychological skills. Most of
them, on the other hand, *did* mention the time pressures of a busy
practice, although they were aware that, in principle, trouble taken
early on might save a lot of time in the long run, since it may prevent
a problem escalating over the years. However, doctors are often not
able to apply this important insight in their own practice.

But it would be unfair to lay the blame entirely on doctors for the
primary health service's failure in dealing with these disorders.
Many of the underlying problems are in areas beyond the doctor's
jurisdiction – housing, employment, crime, education, poverty, the
struggle to survive against mechanistic, materialistic and often
hostile social forces. Doctors, as we have said, ought to be more
aware of the resources which are available to help people cope with
these, but medicine does not change the basic conditions of life. In
any case, the medicine which doctors practice is itself a product of
these forces. Multinational modern medicine is based on the same
basic process as multinational industry, that of using technology to
sell the idea of limitless economic growth and 'improvement' of the
planet. Doctors are as much sold on the dream of ever-better ways
of intervening in the body as the rest of us are on ever-better cars
and hi-fi equipment. Our age is one in which nature is something
to be transformed almost at any cost, and few of us are not in some
way implicated.

The anxieties and neuroses caused by this pressure for an
increasingly 'unnatural' world help to breed the compulsions with
which we have been concerned in this book, and tend to make
compulsive consumers of us all. The fact that medicine and medical
training are themselves a part of this pressure is manifestly
unhelpful: what is needed is a *new* medicine, capable of more than
a sigh of regret and a tranquilliser prescription.

A New Medicine

A new medicine would be, in some ways, a very old medicine, or at least a better blend of the ancient and the new. The 'father' of medicine, Hippocrates, said that it was more important to discover what kind of person has a disease than to know what kind of disease a person has. He might have been outlining the holistic view of medicine which is gaining ground today amongst 'alternative' practitioners. For the treatment of compulsive disorders, at least, a wider application of this philosophy would appear to be urgently needed.

The ancient theory of medicine, in the Hippocratic tradition, was based on the notion that the person as a whole needed to be in balance or, if you think in musical terms, in harmony. Harmony, like perspective, is partly a science and partly an art, and medicine is the same. Unless doctors can see people as whole rather than as a collection of organs and symptoms, they will miss the way in which disorders make the whole life of a person discordant. Just as you cannot evaluate a musical note without reference to other notes played before, during and after it, so you cannot judge a symptom in isolation.

This is why it is nonsense to try to treat an alcoholic solely by a process of drying out, a heroin addict by 'cold turkey' or an anorexic by force-feeding. Unless they *understand* where their compulsive behaviour comes from and where it is placed in relation to the whole of their lives, their treatment is bound to be ineffective.

Recovery from compulsion is a process of learning, but it is not the type of learning recommended by Professor Eysenck (quoted on page 4). The behaviourist's learning is a passive process, whereas holistic learning is active and voluntary. Even to learn and to reject the conclusion, as the anorexic Catherine Dunbar seems to have done, is an individual's prerogative. Contrary to the wisdom of materialistic medicine, even a death is not necessarily a medical tragedy.

Such ideas do not come easily to modern medicine, but they are necessary if improvements are to be made in the treatment of psychological disorders, among which compulsions feature so heavily.

Community Support and Change

We hope we have made it clear throughout that these compulsions should not be seen as problems that face *other people*. We all have experiences of compulsive behaviour, and under pressure any of us may face the kind of problems described by the sufferers and their families in this book.

The community as a whole therefore shares a responsibility to face up to the causes, whether national or local, which create these problems or make them worse. We have seen that in some cases, like alcohol or tranquilliser addiction, easy availability is an encouragement. Similarly the marketing strategies of drinks, tobacco and drug companies can exploit people's vulnerabilities and profit from their compulsions. The huge revenues from taxation on alcohol are spent, directly and indirectly, entirely on repairing the damage alcohol causes, a fact which speaks for itself. But although charities like Alcohol Concern and MIND put pressure on the government to shape more effective policies in these areas, they need a much larger measure of public support if they are to be successful.

There is a distinct lack of coordination between government departments and the agencies on the ground. Most compulsions involve major social as well as medical problems, and yet there is often no liaison between health and social services over them. At the same time, as we have heard repeatedly, there are not nearly enough resources devoted to research and support: indeed the shortage of crisis facilities for drug addicts, and the lack of follow-up for what does exist, is a national scandal. It is a sad irony that, in a democracy which places such a high value on *choice*, we are not prepared to give more help to people who have become trapped in circles of compulsion and, in the process, have lost their freedom to choose.

But it is all too easy to blame government policies and do nothing ourselves. We have tried to stress the importance of changing our own attitudes to mental health problems and our relationship to the medical establishment. Many compulsive sufferers feel they lack control over their lives; we can all try to take positive control over our health, both mental and physical, instead of handing over the reins to an authority figure like a doctor. This means actively trying to learn about prevention: stress-management, ways to relax, the appreciation of the meaning and quality of our lives, the dangers of perfectionism and becoming too narrowly focused on particular goals. By learning to deal with our problems as and when they arise without trying to mask them, and to help each other to do so, we can avoid trouble in the future.

Compulsive behaviour has, above all, the characteristic that it *shuts other people out,* which means it is not just bad for communities and families, but must be recognised as a product of them. Therefore compulsion will only be effectively prevented if action is taken at all levels of society. We can begin by recognising that we have it in our power to make changes in the way we live with ourselves and with each other.

Changing your Life

Four of the six compulsions we have discussed are centred on perfectly normal activities which all of us do, or have done. It is sometimes not easy to recognise when the normal is beginning to spill over into the compulsive, and for each of these four compulsions we have compiled ten early warning signs to look out for. But remember that these are only *signs*. If one or two of them occasionally apply to you, it is probably nothing to worry about. If, however, three or more of them occur regularly, you should consider whether you might have a problem.

Warning Signs For Compulsive Eating

- Spending much time thinking about food and planning what to eat or how to diet;
- constantly worrying about how you look, and about feeling too fat in spite of your friends' assurances that you are not;
- avidly reading anything to do with dieting and eating and constantly trying new diets and diet foods;
- feeling nervous and unsure of your ability to control your food intake;
- preferring to eat alone, even secretly, rather than with the family or in public;
- when eating in company, pretending to eat more than you do and hiding the uneaten food;
- finding it impossible to stop eating some foods (e.g. chocolate or ice cream) until your supply has run out;
- feeling self-disgust when you have eaten, on the grounds that you are becoming fat through over-eating;
- taking excessive exercise.

Warning Signs for Compulsive Drinking

- Planning and looking forward to your next drink;

- drinking faster than other people
- feeling nervous if there is no alcohol on hand;
- feeling you cannot enjoy an occasion without alcohol;
- drinking every day and often feeling below par in the morning;
- using drink as a pick-me-up, a confidence booster or when you are unhappy;
- believing you are better company, or perform better socially and at work, after a drink;
- being nervous or angry if someone suggests you are drinking too much;
- finding it hard to refuse when a drink is offered, even though you think you have had enough;
- sometimes regretting things you have said during a drinking session – or not *remembering* what you may have said.

Warning Signs for Workaholics

- Often feeling wound-up and finding it hard to *un*wind;
- seeing work as the most important aspect of your life, above family and friends;
- always having work with you, thinking about work and finding it difficult to switch it off;
- being reluctant to take time off for weekends or holidays;
- if you do take time off, phoning the office repeatedly or feeling generally ill at ease;
- hating to delegate;
- trying to save time by doing several work activities at once;
- making mistakes at work because of hurrying;
- becoming unreasonably impatient in queues or slow moving traffic;
- using work as an excuse to avoid family or social responsibilities.

Warning Signs for Compulsive Love or Jealousy

- Having a history of several unhappy relationships;
- repeatedly being attracted to the same type of person;
- feeling tense and anxious about the present relationship;
- feeling the other person has all the power and you are 'at their mercy';
- neglecting family, friends and interests which are otherwise important to you;
- not wanting the other person to have outside friendships or

interests;

- feeling that time spent apart is wasted time, and obsessively preparing for the next meeting;
- being insecure about the other person's feelings for you, even though he or she expresses love and reassurance;
- not believing anyone could love you if they 'found out' what you were really like;
- feeling you want to 'own' or over-protect the other person.

Where to Get Help

This book has stressed that, if you suffer from a compulsion, it is important to tackle the underlying problems which have led you to 'choose' that behaviour, and to start sorting out those problems.

To take one example, suppose you are having trouble getting to sleep because you look after young children in inadequate housing conditions. Suppose, at the same time, you are worried about money and, for more than three months, you have been taking tranquillisers to help you cope with these problems. At the same time as finding out how to come off the pills (perhaps by contacting a self-help group), see what you can do about the child care, housing and money problems. This may involve getting advice from a Housing Aid Centre or tenants' organisation, seeing if there are any daytime child-care facilities (such as a playgroup) in your area, contacting a debt counselling service, or anyone who will give you detailed advice about money worries.

Taking practical steps such as these may seem very hard when you are feeling low and isolated, but it is very important to do so. Your local Citizen's Advice Bureau can point you in the right directions, if they cannot help directly. Never be intimidated or ashamed to ask for a particular piece of advice – you certainly will not be the first or last to need it.

This book is about improving the quality of our lives, not just giving up things which are bad for us. Even if you do succeed in stopping the tranquillisers, you should sort out these problems, or you may find yourself resorting to another compulsion (such as alcohol). Never underestimate the importance of making practical changes. Doing something active will also help the isolation which goes with many compulsions.

Finally *start today*. Unhappy situations usually do not improve by themselves or by 'waiting and seeing', and the longer they are left, the worse they can become. We spoke to so many people who have succeeded in changing their lives, and whose only regret is that it took them years to seek help. As we were told be Gayle, who was hooked on heroin for fifteen years and could not imagine life without the drug: 'You *can* change your life. There *is* life without junk. There is hope.'

We hope the following lists of organisations will help in taking that first step.

General Organisations

**Association of Community
Health Councils** (01) 272 5459
Mark Lemon Suite
254 Seven Sisters Rd
London N4 2HZ
Community Health Councils are a network of information centres for local health facilities and will help with problems with GPs.

**Association of Self-Help and
Community Groups** (01) 579 5589
7 Chesham St
London W13 9HX

Citizens Advice Bureaux
See telephone directories.

Contact (0232) 57848
2a Ribble St
Newtonwards Rd
Belfast
Telephone and walk-in advice centre for young people.

**Institute for Complementary
Medicine** (01) 636 9543
21 Portland Place
London W1N 2AF
Will tell you about alternatives to orthodox medical treatment, and where to find them.

LINK Glasgow Association for
  Mental Health   (041) 332 2541
2 Queen's Crescent   (041) 332 3186
Glasgow G4 9BW
Free counselling.

Maudsley Hospital   (01) 703 6333
Denmark Hill
London SE5 8AZ
Emergency, 24-hour, walk-in clinic for people with urgent problems.

MIND   (01) 637 0741
22 Harley St
London W1N 2ED
*MIND is the National Association for Mental Health. It offers
information on all aspects of mental health and has regional offices.*

**National Association of Young People's
  Counselling and Advice Services**   (0533) 554775
17-23 Albion St   ext. 22 and 36
Leicester LE1 6GD
Information on local services.

**Northern Ireland Association of
  Mental Health**   (0232) 228474
Beacon House
84 University St
Belfast BT7 1HE
Advice service.

Women's Heath Information Centre   (01) 251 6580
52 Fetherstone St
London EC1Y 8RT

Problem Eating

Anorexic Aid   (0494) 21431
The Priory Centre
11 Priory Rd
High Wycombe
Bucks
National self-help groups.

Anorexic Family Aid   (0603) 621414
Sackville Place
44 Magdalen St
Norwich
NR3 1JE

The Women's Therapy Centre   (01) 263 6200
6 Manor Gardens
London N7

Overeaters Anonymous   (01) 868 4109

**The Society for the Advancement
  of Research into Anorexia**   (0403) 700210
Stanthorpe New Pound
Wisborough Green
Billingshurst
West Sussex

Problem Drinking

There are hundreds of different organisations for problem drinkers, and we list just a few contacts which will help you to locate services in your area.

Accept   (01) 381 3157
200 Seagrave Rd
London SW6
Accept *also houses* Drinkwatchers, *which promotes sensible drinking.*

Action on Alcohol Abuse   (01) 222 3454
11 Carteret St
London SW1H 9DL

Al-Anon   (01) 403 0888
61 Great Dover St
London S1 4YF
For relatives and friends of problem drinkers.

Alcohol Concern   (01) 833 3471
305 Gray's Inn Rd
London WC1 8QF

Compulsion

Alcoholics Anonymous
In Greater London   (01) 352 9669
Outside London   (0904) 644026

Greater London Alcohol
   Advisory Service (GLAAS)   (01) 248 8406
For information about local groups in the London area.

Hospital Treatment Centres
Many hospitals have alcohol units: your doctor or one of the organisations listed here will be able to put you in touch with them.

Northern Ireland Council on
   Alcohol   (0232) 664434
40 Elmwood Avenue
Belfast BT9 6AZ

Scottish Council on Alcohol   (041) 333 9677
137 Sauchiehall St
Glasgow G2 3EW

TACADE
Teacher's Advisory Council on
   Alcohol and Drug Education
2 Mount St
Manchester M2 5NG
Develops material for schools; also available to the public.

Women's Alcohol Centre   (01) 226 4581
253 St Paul's Rd
London N1

Tranquillisers

See also General Organisations.

Gateway Project   (031) 661 0982
2-4 Abbeymount
Edinburgh

TRANX   (01) 427 2065
17 Peel Rd   (01) 427 2827
Wealdstone
Harrow
Middlesex HA3 7QX
Offering therapy, telephone advice and a national referral service.

Withdraw Project   (021) 378 2211
Highcroft Hospital
Highcroft Rd
Erdington, Birmingham
An NHS project, offering therapy and counselling.

Heroin

The agencies listed in this section will advise on use of other drugs as well as heroin.

Angel Project   (01) 226 3113
38-44 Liverpool Rd
London N1
Telephone counselling.

City Roads   (01) 278 8671
358 City Road   (01) 278 8672
London EC1
Crisis intervention, with short stay detoxification and telephone advice.

**Department of Health and
   Social Security**
Dept DM
DHSS Leaflet Unit
PO Box 21
   Information leaflets for parents and teachers about drug abuse.

Drugline   (01) 291 2341
28 Ballina St
London SE23 1DR
Telephone advice for parents.

Families Anonymous   (01) 278 8805
88 Caledonian Rd
London N1 9DN
Support groups for the families of drug users, along the lines of Alcoholics Anonymous.

Institute for the Study of
   Drug Dependence   (01) 430 1991
1-4 Hatton Place
Hatton Garden
London EC1N 8ND
Independent body which runs an information service.

National Association of Family
   Support Groups
c/o Merseyside Family Support Group
New Zealand House
18 Water St
Liverpool 1
Will help you make contact with a local group.

Phoenix House   (01) 699 5748
1 Elliot Bank
Forest Hill, Lewisham
London SE23
Long-stay therapy.

Release   (01) 603 8654
Sympathetic emergency advice (24 hours) about medical, social and legal problems.

SCODA
Standing Conference on Drug Abuse   (01) 430 2341
1-4 Hatton Place
Hatton Garden
London EC1N 8ND
National coordinating body giving information about specialist agencies.

TACADE
Teacher's Advisory Council on
Alcohol and Drug Education
2 Mount St
Manchester M2 5NG
Develops material for schools; also available to the public.

Work

These organisations offer help and advice for workaholics, including stress management and relaxation techniques.

Coronary Prevention Group   (01) 833 3687
60 Great Ormond St
London WC1N 3HR

**Coronary-Prone Behaviour
   Research Unit**   (061) 228 6171
Dept of Biological Sciences
Manchester Polytechnic
Chester St
Manchester M1 5GD

**International Stress and Tension
   Control Society**   (01) 876 8261
The Priory Hospital
Priory Lane
Roehampton
Surrey SW15 5JJ

Lifestyle Training Centre Ltd   (01) 938 1011
23 Abingdon Rd
London W8
Produces cassettes on anxiety and stress management.

Positive Health Centre   (01) 935 1811
101 Harley St
London W1

Relaxation for Living
29 Burwood Park Rd
Walton-On-Thames
Surrey K212 5LM

The Relaxation Society   (01) 626 9701
St Mary Woolnoth Church
Lombard St
London EC3V 9AN
A general health promotion group, which has regular lunch-time relaxation sessions in the City of London.

The Stress Clinic   (01) 703 6333
The Maudsley Hospital
Denmark Hill
London SE5

Relationships

See also General Organisations, many of which will be able to advise on where to go for help.

**Association of Sexual and
   Marital Therapists**
PO Box 62
Sheffield S10 3TL
Information and referral for married and single people.

Brook Advisory Centres   (01) 708 1234
153a East St
London SE17 2SD
A nationwide network of counselling services for people under 25 on sexual and emotional problems.

National Marriage Guidance Council   (0788) 73241
Herbert Gray College
Little Church St
Rugby
Warwickshire CV21 3AP
Marriage Guidance Councils exist all over the country, and will counsel married or unmarried couples; for local details contact the national office or consult a telephone directory.

Changing your Life

Scottish Marriage Guidance Council   (031) 225 5006
26 Frederick St
Edinburgh EH2 2JR

Other Specialist Organisations

**Crisis Counselling for Alleged
   Shoplifters**   (01) 202 5787
Emergency telephone counselling.

Gamblers Anonymous   (01) 352 3060
17/23 Blantyre St
Cheyne Walk
London SW10 0DT

**Institute for the Study
   and Treatment of Delinquency**   (01) 680 2068
34 Surrey St
Croydon
CR0 1RJ

NACRO   (01) 582 6500
National Association for Care
   and Resettlement of Offenders
169 Clapham Rd
London SW9 0PU

Portia Trust   (0900) 812114
15 Senhouse St
Cumbria CA15 6AB
Helps women who have committed crimes through emotional disturbance.

A Final Note. Many of these organisations are charities for whom postal costs are a heavy burden. So if you write for information, please enclose a stamped addressed envelope.